good cooking

Delicious Desserts

Published by:

R&R Publications Marketing Pty. Ltd

ACN 083 612 579

PO Box 254, Carlton North, Victoria 3054 Australia

Phone (61 3) 9381 2199 Fax (61 3) 9381 2689

E-mail: info@randrpublications.com.au

Web: www.randrpublications.com.au

© Richard Carroll

Good Cooking Delicious Desserts

Publisher: Richard Carroll

Creative Director: Lucy Adams

Production Manager: Anthony Carroll

Computer Graphics: Lucy Adams

Food Photography: Steve Baxter, Phillip Wilkins, David Munns, Thomas Odulate, Christine Hanscomb, Gary Smith, Warren Webb and Frank Wieder

Home Economist: Sara Buenfeld, Emma Patmore, Nancy McDougall, Louise Pickford, Jane Stevenson, Oded Schwartz, Alison Austin and Jane Lawrie

Food Stylists: Helen Payne, Sue Russell, Sam Scott, Antonia Gaunt Ellen Argyriou and Oded Schwartz

Recipe Development: Terry Farris, Jacqueline Bellefontaine, Ellen Argyriou Becky Johnson, Valerie Barrett, Emma Patmore, Geri Richards, Pam Mallender, Jan Fullwood and Tamara Milstein (www. tamaraskitchen.com) 99, 100, 106, 148, 156, 158, 163, 164, 176, 210, 246, 252, 300, 314, 316, 318, 324, 328, 330, 332.

Nutritional Consultant: Moya de Wet BSc SRD

Proof Reader: Lily Green

Includes Index

ISBN 1 74022 224 5

EAN 9 781740 222242

First Edition Printed

Computer Typeset in Times New Roman, Verdana, Helvetica, Shelley Allegro & Humanist

Printed in Singapore by Saik Wah Press Pte Ltd

good cooking

Contents

Delicious Desserts

Who doesn't love desserts! Everyone does, but how many of us are confident about selecting an appropriate dessert for an occasion and preparing the dessert we have selected? At one time or another, we all have to make a dessert and, of course, we want to present to our family and friends a final course that looks stunning and tastes delicious yet does not involve hours of work. Now, you no longer need to worry. With Delicious Desserts, you will quickly discover how easy and enjoyable making desserts can be. And the results will speak for themselves – your family and friends will be delighted!

There are many occasions when you may need to prepare a dessert. Delicious Desserts offers to you a vast array of final course choices for your pleasure. You will find something here for every occasion. From something simple, sweet and wholesome for the family to a decadent, heavenly chocolate creation designed to impress – you will find a dessert to suit all tastes, budgets, and events. There are lots of simple treats using what you have already got in your pantry, plus new and stunning creations featuring special ingredients or techniques. All recipes use the freshest and best ingredients and are inspired by today's busy lifestyle. And each recipe is enhanced by a stunning photograph that suggest ways to serve the dish and what accompaniments to offer.

Delicious Desserts is divided into clearly marked sections for easy use. There are recipes for simple treats, summer and autumn favorites, winter favorites, chocolate, and special occasions. All recipes have easy-to-follow instructions, and many have a note providing you with an interesting fact or suggestion to extend the recipe and your knowledge of food and cooking.

Delicious Desserts will ensure you are equipped to prepare the right dessert for any occasion. The recipes will satisfy and impress your guests and, above all, encourage you to enjoy entertaining and approach any special occasion with confidence. Allow this book to become an important part of your cooking library – your family and friends will love you for it!

In this section, you will find delicious yet simple desserts to tempt family and friends when you don't have much time or a stocked pantry. Learn how to use simple ingredients for spectacular results.

Simple Treats

Simple Treats

Apple Roll-Ups

Ingredients

2 oz/55 g all-purpose flour

5½ fl oz/150 mL whole milk

1 medium egg

finely grated rind of ½ small orange

1 oz/30 g butter, melted,
  plus extra for frying

maple syrup and heavy cream
  to serve

Filling

2 eating apples, peeled,
  cored, and chopped

½ tsp ground cinnamon

1 To make the batter, blend the flour, milk, egg, orange rind, and melted butter until smooth in a food processor or using a hand blender. Leave to rest for 20 minutes.

Method

2 Meanwhile, make the filling. Put the apples, cinnamon, and 1 tablespoon of water into a small saucepan, cover, and cook gently for 5–7 minutes, stirring occasionally, until the apples have softened.

3 Melt just enough butter to cover the base of a 7 in/18 cm non-stick frying pan. Pour in a ¼ of the batter and tilt the pan so that it covers the base. Cook for 1–2 minutes on each side, until golden. Keep warm and repeat to make 3 more pancakes, greasing the pan when necessary.

4 Place 2 pancakes on each plate. Fill with the apple filling and carefully roll up. Serve with the maple syrup and a dollop of heavy cream.

Serves 2

Apple, Pear, and Banana Crumble

Ingredients

2 dessert apples, peeled and sliced

2 ripe pears, peeled, cored, and sliced

3 tbsp apple juice

1 tbsp clear honey

2 bananas, sliced

Topping

4 oz/115 g butter, cut into cubes

5 oz/145 g all-purpose flour

$^1/_3$ cup raw sugar

Method

1 Preheat the oven to 400°F/200°C/Gas Mark 6. Place the apples and pears in a large, shallow, ovenproof dish, add the apple juice, and drizzle over the honey. Lay the bananas on top.

2 Rub the butter into the flour, using your fingertips, until the mixture resembles rough breadcrumbs. Stir in the sugar and spoon this mixture over the bananas.

3 Cook for 30–35 minutes or until the fruit is bubbling and the topping is golden.

Serves 4

Almond Barfi

Ingredients

8 oz/225 g blanched almonds

1/2 cup milk

4oz/115g sugar

1/2 cup water

14oz/400g can condensed milk

6 oz/170 g butter, diced

Decoration

silver leaf, optional

**1/4 cup pistachio nuts, shelled
    and roughly chopped**

Method

1 Grease a 10 in x8 in/25 cm x20 cm baking tin. Grind the almonds with a little of the milk in a blender or food processor to make a rough paste. Add the remaining milk and process briefly to mix.

2 Put the sugar and measured water in a heavy-based saucepan. Stir over a gentle heat until the sugar has dissolved. Increase the heat and boil rapidly until the mixture registers 235°F/115°C/Gas Mark 1/4 on a sugar thermometer stage.

3 Stir the almond mixture and condensed milk into the syrup. Add butter and stir until fully dissolved.

4 Bring the mixture to the boil again and boil until it again registers 235°F/115°C/Gas Mark 1/4, the 'soft ball' stage.

5 Pour the barf mixture into the prepared tin, and spread evenly. Carefully lay the silver leaf on top, if using, then sprinkle with the pistachio nuts. Cool, then refrigerate overnight to set.

6 Allow the barfi to return to room temperature before cutting into squares or diamonds to serve.

Makes about 30 pieces

Apple and Date Ricotta Slice

Ingredients

1 ½ cups whole-wheat
all-purpose flour
½ tsp baking powder
2oz/55g butter or margarine
½ cup superfine sugar
¼–⅓ cup iced water

Apple Date Topping
14 oz/400 g canned pie apple, drained
⅓ cup fresh or dried dates, pitted
   and halved
1 lb/455 g ricotta cheese, drained
½ cup superfine sugar
2 tbsp flour
½ cup reduced-fat milk
2 eggs, lightly beaten
1 tbsp brandy

Method

1 Place the flour and butter in a food processor and process until the mixture resembles fine breadcrumbs. Add the sugar and process to combine. With the machine running, slowly add enough water to form a rough dough. Turn the dough onto a lightly floured surface and knead briefly. Wrap the dough in plastic wrap and refrigerate for 20 minutes.

2 Roll out the dough to ¼ in/5 mm thick and large enough to line the base of a lightly greased and lined 9 in/23 cm square cake tin.

3 To make the apple date topping, arrange the apples and dates over the pastry. Place the ricotta cheese, sugar, flour, milk, eggs and brandy in a bowl and beat until smooth. Spoon the ricotta mixture over the fruit, spread out evenly and bake for 1 hour or until the topping is set. Cool in the tin, then cut into square to serve.

Makes 36

Baked Fresh Dates and Apples

Ingredients

5 large cooking apples

butter, for greasing

7 oz/200 g dates, fresh, stoned, and halved

juice of 1/2 lemon

juice of 2 oranges

rind of 1 orange, finely grated

2 cinnamon quills

3 tbsp clear honey

plain yogurt, to serve

ground cinnamon, to garnish

Method

1 Preheat the oven to 350°F/180°C/Gas Mark 4.

2 Peel and slice the apples thinly. Place in a shallow oven-proof dish greased with the butter. Stir in the dates, juices, rind and cinnamon quills. Drizzle the honey over the mixture.

3 Cover and bake for 45–55 minutes until tender and the flavors are absorbed.

4 Serve warm or chilled with the plain yogurt, dusted with the cinnamon.

Serves 4

Banana Fritters

Ingredients

vegetable oil for deep-frying

**4 large firm bananas, cut in $1/2$,
then split lengthways**

2 tbsp lime juice

Batter

1 cup all-purpose flour

1 tsp baking powder

2 tbsp superfine sugar

$1/2$ cup milk

1 egg, lightly beaten

1 egg white

Caramel Sauce

$1/2$ cup brown or palm sugar

$1/2$ cup water

$1/2$ cup heavy cream

2 tsp whisky, optional

Method

1 To make the batter, sift the flour in a bowl and make a well in the center. Combine the superfine sugar, milk, and egg, then mix into the flour mixture to make a batter of a smooth consistency. Stand for 10 minutes.

2 To make the caramel sauce, place the sugar and water in a saucepan and cook over a low heat, stirring constantly, until the sugar dissolves. Bring to the boil, then reduce the heat and simmer, without stirring, for 5 minutes or until the mixture is golden. Remove the sauce pan from the heat and carefully stir in cream and whisky, if using. Return the pan to a low heat and cook, stirring, until combined. Cool.

3 Beat the egg white until soft peaks form, then fold into the batter. Heat the oil in a saucepan until a cube of bread dropped in browns in 50 seconds. Brush the bananas with the lime juice dip in the batter to coat then drain off the excess. Cook the bananas in the hot oil for 2–3 minutes or until golden. Serve immediately with the caramel sauce.

Serves 4

Coconut Crêpes

Ingredients

$^1/_2$ **cup all-purpose flour**

1 tbsp superfine sugar

2 eggs, lightly beaten

$^3/_4$ **cup milk or coconut milk**

oil spray for cooking

1 cup grated palm sugar or brown sugar

$^1/_2$ **cup water**

1 pandan leaf

1 cup shredded coconut, toasted

1 papaya, diced

wedges of lemon to serve

Method

1   Combine the flour and sugar in a mixing bowl. Add the eggs and milk, and whisk the mixture until smooth. Add a little water if too thick

2 Heat a frying pan. Spray with the oil, then add enough mixture to make a thin crêpes. Cook crêpes for 1–2 minutes on each side.

3   Combine the sugar, water, and pandan leaf in a saucepan. Bring to the boil and simmer over a low heat, stirring stir until the sugar dissolves and the syrup thickens slightly.

4   Place the coconut and papaya on each crêpes and roll up. Serve the crêpes with wedges of lemon and drizzle with the syrup.

Makes 8

Crêpes Suzette with Strawberries

Ingredients

strawberries, sliced
1/2 cup orange juice, warmed
2 tbsp superfine sugar
1 tbsp orange-flavored liqueur
1 tbsp brandy

Crêpes
1 cup all-purpose flour
milk
1/2 cup water
2 eggs
1/2 oz/15g butter, melted
1 tbsp sugar

Method

1 To make the crêpes, place the flour, milk, water, eggs, butter, and sugar in a food processor or blender and process until smooth. Cover and to stand for 1 hour.

2 Pour 2–3 tablespoons of the batter into a heated, lightly greased 7 in/18 cm crêpe pan and tilt the pan so the batter covers the base thinly and evenly. Cook over a high heat for 1 minute or until lightly browned. Turn the crêpe and cook on the other side for 30 seconds. Remove from the pan, set aside, and keep warm. Repeat with the remaining batter to make 12 crêpes.

3 Slice the strawberries and place on the crêpes. Fold the crêpes into 1/4 and arrange, overlapping, in a heatproof dish. Pour the orange juice over and sprinkle with the superfine sugar. Place the orange-flavored liqueur and brandy in a small saucepan and warm over a low heat, ignite, and pour over the crêpes. Serve immediately.

Serves 4

Fried Banana

Ingredients

³/₄ cup rice flour

1 tsp ground cinnamon

1 tsp superfine sugar

²/₃ cup water

3 bananas, peeled

vegetable oil for cooking

lemon wedges to serve

Method

1 Combine the flour, cinnamon, sugar, and water in a mixing bowl. Whisk the mixture together until smooth.

2 Cut the bananas in ¹/₂ lengthways, and then into pieces. Dip the banana pieces in the batter.

3 Heat the oil in a wok or frying pan, add the banana pieces, and cook until golden and crisp. Serve with lemon wedges.

Serves 4

Sweet Bread

Ingredients

**1 loaf of spongy or soft white bread,
preferably round in shape**

**$1/2$ cup sugar (use more
or less depending
on how sweet you like things)**

4 cups milk

6 eggs

olive oil for frying

1 cup sugar, for dusting

$3^1/2$ oz/100 g ground cinnamon

Method

1 Cut the bread into slices about $2^1/2$ cm/1 in thick.

2 Mix the sugar and milk and dip the slices of bread into the mixture. Leave the bread until it is well soaked. Put the slices on a rack or in a colander to drain any surplus liquid.

3 Beat the eggs well and coat the soaked bread on all sides. Heat the oil, which shouldn't be excessively hot, and fry the bread slices until they are golden on all sides. Remove, drain, and sprinkle with the sugar and cinnamon and serve immediately.

Note: Sweet bread can be eaten hot or cold, but they are much better freshly made.

Serves at least 6

Almond Cakes

Ingredients

1 lb/455 g almonds, blanched

1 cup superfine sugar

2 medium eggs

²/₃ oz/20 g soft white bread crumbs

¹/₃ cup liquid honey, warmed

Method

1 Grind the almonds in a food processor with a little of the sugar. Combine the remaining sugar with the eggs, and whisk until pale and creamy. Add the ground almonds to the breadcrumbs, and stir until well combined.

2 Preheat the oven to 350°F/180°C/Gas Mark 4.

3 Shape, using a tablespoon, roughly into diamond shapes, and place on a non-stick baking tray. Bake for 15 minutes.

4 While warm, place the cakes on wire cooling racks, and brush with the warm honey. Leave to cool a little before serving.

Makes 38–40 cakes

American Flapjacks

Ingredients

2 cups all-purpose flour

2 tsp baking powder

1/2 tsp salt

2 tsp sugar

3 eggs

1 1/2 cups milk

dash vanilla essence

3 tbsp melted butter

extra butter to serve

Method

1 Sift the flour and salt together into a bowl and sprinkle over the sugar. Heat the eggs, milk, and vanilla together and pour over the flour. Stir until just blended. The batter will be lumpy. Stir in the melted butter.

2 Heat a heavy, greased frying pan or griddle until a drop of cold water, flicked on to the surface, bounces and splutters. Put the batter on in spoonfuls, a little distance apart, and cook until bubbles appear on the surface and the undersides are lightly browned. Turn and brown the other sides. Serve in a stack with butter in between.

Makes 18–20 hotcakes.

Banana Drama

Ingredients

1 oz/30 g butter

1 eating apple, peeled, cored and sliced

2 bananas, sliced thickly

finely grated rind of ¹/₄ lemon and ¹/₂ tsp lemon juice

1 oz/30 g soft light brown sugar

¹/₄ tsp ground cinnamon

ice cream to serve

Method

1   Melt the butter in a medium-sized saucepan. Add the apple and cook over a medium heat for 3 minutes, turning once, until softened. Add the bananas, stir gently, and cook for a further 2 minutes or until golden.

2   Add the lemon rind and juice, sugar and cinnamon to the sauce pan. Cook for 2–3 minutes, stirring gently, until the sauce turns golden and coats the fruit. Serve immediately with ice cream.

Serves 2

Frozen Mango Blush

Ingredients

2 large mangos, diced and frozen,
  about 2 cups mango flesh

4 strawberries

1¼ cups low-fat yogurt of your
  choice natural, passionfruit
  or apricot all work well
  for this dessert

1–2 tbsp orange juice or
  sparkling wine

Method

1 Allow the mangos to soften slightly (so you don't ruin the blades of your food processor), then place in a food processor. Add the strawberries and yogurt.

2 Using the pulse button, process to combine. With the motor running, slowly add the orange juice. Process until the desired consistency is achieved. Serve immediately or freeze and serve as a refreshing summer ice.

Serves 4

Hazelnut Crêpes with Strawberries

Ingredients

4 medium eggs

¹/₂ cup half-fat milk

3 tbsp clear honey or sugar

3¹/₂ oz/100 g roasted chopped hazelnuts

3¹/₂ oz/100 g all-purpose flour

1 tsp baking powder

1 tsp ground cinnamon

pinch of salt

3 tbsp melted butter

³/₄ cup maple syrup

4 fl oz/115 g tub clotted cream

a few strawberries

Method

1 Beat the eggs with the milk and honey or sugar until light and fluffy. Gradually add the hazelnuts, flour, baking powder, cinnamon, and salt, then beat to a smooth batter.

2 Heat a small, heavy-based frying pan, then brush with 1 teaspoon of the melted butter. Drop in 2 tablespoons of the batter, then quickly tilt the pan to cover the base. Fry for 1–2 minutes, until golden, turn over and fry for a further minute or until browned. Repeat until all the batter has been used (it makes about 18 crêpes), greasing the pan as necessary.

3 Serve the crêpes drizzled with the maple syrup and topped with the clotted cream and strawberries.

Serves 6

Hop Scotch

Ingredients

3 1/3 oz/100 g butterscotch candy

1 lb/455 g tub vanilla ice cream

10 1/2 fl oz/300 g can mandarins, drained

3 chocolate flakes

Method

1 Put the butterscotch candy into a strong plastic bag. Roughly crush with a rolling pin.

2 Place the ice cream in a large bowl and mash with a fork. Mix in the crushed butterscotch. Return to the container and freeze for 1–2 hours.

3 Transfer the ice cream to the refridgerator for 20 minutes before serving to soften slightly. Place the mandarins in sundae glasses, together with 2 scoops of ice cream. Crush one of the chocolate flakes and sprinkle over the top of the ice cream. Cut the remaining flakes in half and push 1 into each serving.

Serves 4

Hot Bananas with Caramel Sauce

Ingredients

½ oz/15 g butter

2 tbsp superfine sugar

**4 large bananas, peeled and each
  cut into 3 pieces**

4 fl oz/115 mL double cream

Method

1 Place the butter in a large heavy-based frying pan over a medium heat. As soon as the butter has melted, sprinkle over the sugar. Cook for 1–2 minutes, or until the sugar begins to bubble and turn dark golden, taking care not to let it burn.

2 Quickly add the banana pieces to the caramel and toss to coat. Reduce the heat a little and cook for 1 minute, or until the caramel is bubbling. Pour in the cream and stir for a further minute to mix thoroughly and heat through the banana pieces.

Serves 4

Mixed Fruit Compote

Ingredients

1 cup fresh rhubarb, chopped

¼ cup soft light brown sugar

**14 oz/400 g mixed ready-to-eat
dried fruit, such as apricots,
peaches, apples, and pears, cut
into even-sized pieces**

Method

1 Preheat the oven to 350°F/180°C/Gas Mark 4.
Place the rhubarb in a saucepan with the sugar and
½ pint/300 mL water. Simmer for 5 minutes or until
the fruit begins to soften.

2 Place the dried fruit in an ovenproof dish, add the
rhubarb and its cooking liquid and stir gently.

3 Cover the dish and bake for 20–25 minutes,
stirring halfway through cooking, until the fruit has
softened. Serve warm or chilled.

Serves 4

New Orleans-Style Bananas

Ingredients

2 oz/55 g sweet butter

¼ cup brown sugar

½ tsp ground cinnamon

¼ cup banana-flavored
liqueur or orange juice

½ cup dark rum

4 bananas, halved lengthwise

4 scoops vanilla ice cream

Method

1 Melt the butter in a heavy-based saucepan over a medium heat, add the sugar and cinnamon, and cook, stirring, until the sugar melts and the mixture is combined.

2 Stir in the liqueur or orange juice and ½ the rum, and cook for 5 minutes or until the mixture is thick and syrupy.

3 Add the bananas and toss to coat with the syrup. Add the remaining rum, swirl the pan, and ignite immediately. Baste the bananas with the sauce until the flame goes out.

4 To serve, divide the bananas and ice cream between serving plates and drizzle the sauce from pan over the ice cream.

Serves 4

Parsnip Passion

Ingredients

1 cup all-purpose flour,
  plus 1 tsp baking powder
3 oz/85 g superfine sugar
3 oz/85 g soft light brown sugar
1 tsp baking powder
1 tsp bicarbonate of soda
1/2 tsp ground cinnamon
1/2 tsp salt
1/2 cup sunflower oil
2 medium eggs, beaten
1/2 cup parsnip, grated
7 oz/200 g canned crushed
  pineapple, drained

Icing

10 oz/285 g confectioners'
  sugar, sifted
1/2 cup mascarpone
4 tsp lemon juice
2 drops vanilla essence
1 box colored fondant icing

Method

1 Preheat the oven to 350°F/180°C/Gas Mark 4. Using a wooden spoon, combine the flour, superfine and brown sugar, baking powder, bicarbonate of soda, cinnamon and salt. Add the oil and eggs and beat until thoroughly combined. Mix in the parsnips and pineapple and beat well.

2 Spoon the mixture into paper cases in 2 bun trays and bake for 15–20 minutes, until firm and golden. Cool for a few minutes, then remove from the trays and set aside for 30 minutes or until cool. Meanwhile, make the icing. Mix the confectioners' sugar, mascarpone, lemon juice, and vanilla essence with a fork until smooth. Spread over the cakes.

3 Cut out mini parsnip shapes from the yellow fondant icing. Pare strips of green fondant with a vegetable peeler, then twist round a clean pencil to curl. Gently slip the curls off the pencil and set aside to dry. Arrange the parsnips on top of the cakes.

Serves 4

Passionfruit and Mango Granita

Ingredients

2 passionfruit

1¼ cup fresh orange juice

juice of 1 lemon

2 tbsp clear honey

1 ripe mango

Method

1 Halve the passionfruit, then scoop out the pulp and seeds, and place in a small saucepan with the orange and lemon juice and honey. Bring to the boil and cook for 1 minute, stirring, or until the honey dissolves. Leave to cool for 20 minutes.

2 Peel the mango and cut off 8 thin slices. Wrap them in plastic wrap and place in the refrigerator. Chop the remaining mango flesh and blend with the passionfruit mixture in a food processor or using a hand blender – the mixture should be fairly smooth but the seeds should remain whole.

3 Pour the mixture into a freezer container and freeze for 2 hours, whisking once or twice to break up any large ice crystals, then freeze for a further 1 hour or until the mixture crystallizes. Serve the granita in small glasses, each one topped with 2 mango slices.

Serves 4

The Easiest Apple Pie

Ingredients

9 oz/255 g all-purpose flour

4 oz/115 g butter, cubed

2 tbsp apricot jelly

1 lb/455 g cooking apples, peeled, cored, and thinly sliced

1 tsp ground cinnamon

1/2 tsp mixed spice

finely grated rind of 1 orange

1/4 cup soft light brown sugar

1/4 cup golden raisins

confectioners' sugar to dust

Method

1 Preheat the oven to 375°F/190°C/Gas Mark 5. Put the flour into a bowl and rub in the butter until the mixture resembles fine breadcrumbs. Add enough cold water (about 3–4 tablespoons) to make a smooth dough. Knead very lightly.

2 Roll out the pastry to a 14 in/35 cm round on a lightly floured surface. Place on a large baking sheet. Spread the jelly over the center of the pastry. In a bowl, toss together the apples, cinnamon, mixed spice, grated orange rind, sugar and golden raisins, then pile the mixture into the middle of the pastry. Bring the edges of the pastry up over the apple mixture, pressing into rough pleats but leaving the center of the pie open.

3 Bake for 35–45 minutes, until the pastry is golden, covering the pie with foil if the apple starts to burn. Remove the foil, if using, then sprinkle over the confectioners' sugar before serving.

Serves 4

In this section, you will find desserts that use the bounty of these two stunning seasons — Summer and Fall. In Summer, berries are abundant — learn how to make the most of them to impress. Fall is a season of mellow fruits, colors, and flavors. Enjoy the tastes of Fall with these desserts.

Summer and Fall Favorites

Summer and Fall Favorites

Watermelon with Lime Syrup

Ingredients

grated rind and juice of 1 lime

1 oz/30 g superfine sugar

2¼ lb/1 kg watermelon

1 tbsp finely shredded mint

Method

1 Place the lime juice in a small saucepan with the superfine sugar. Stir over a low heat to dissolve the sugar, then boil for 1 minute or until reduced to a syrupy consistency. Pour into a jug and cool for 20 minutes, then refrigerate for 1 hour or overnight.

2 Cut the skin from the watermelon, then remove and discard the seeds. Cut the flesh into bite-size chunks, catching any juices in a bowl. Sprinkle the watermelon chunks with the mint and toss them together lightly.

3 Add the reserved melon juice to the chilled syrup and pour over the melon just before serving. Sprinkle with the grated lime rind.

Serves 4

Earl Grey and Prune Ice Cream

Ingredients

5 Earl Grey tea bags

9 oz/255 g pack ready-to-eat stoned prunes

15 oz/425 g carton ready-to-serve chilled custard

3 tbsp plain yogurt

5 tbsp confectioners' sugar

Sauce

7 tbsp blackcurrant jelly

2 tbsp brandy

2 tbsp plain yogurt

fresh mint to decorate, optional

Method

1 Bring 3 cups of water to the boil in a saucepan, then add the tea bags, stir, and remove from the heat. Leave to infuse for 5 minutes. Lift out the tea bags and bring the liquid to a simmer. Add the prunes and cook for 15 minutes or until softened. Drain, reserving ¼ cup of the liquid.

2 Blend the prunes and the reserved liquid to a purée in a food processor. Mix with the custard, whisking well, then whisk in the yogurt and confectioners' sugar.

3 Pour the mixture into a freezer container. Freeze for 50 minutes, then whisk vigorously and return to the freezer. Repeat after 50 minutes, then leave for 2 hours or until just frozen. Remove from the freezer and leave to soften for 10 minutes.

4 To make the sauce, melt the jelly with 2 tablespoons of water in a small saucepan over a low heat. Add the brandy and simmer for 1 minute. Remove from the heat and stir in the yogurt. Serve the ice cream with the warm sauce spooned over. Decorate with the mint, if using.

Serves 6

Banana Sundae

Ingredients

4 fl oz/115 mL whipping cream

4 small ripe bananas

1²/₃ cups soft-scoop vanilla ice cream

8 tbsp ready-made chocolate sauce

4 tbsp chopped walnuts or mixed chopped nuts

Method

1 Whisk the cream in a bowl until it has thickened and holds its shape when lifted with a spoon – use a balloon whisk or an electric beater.

2 Peel the bananas, slice in half lengthways, and lay in 4 shallow dishes or bowls. Drag a tablespoon along the top of the ice cream to form a ball. Place 2 balls of ice cream between each banana half.

3 Decorate each sundae with ¹/₄ of the whipped cream, 2 tablespoons of the chocolate sauce, and 1 tablespoon of the chopped walnuts. Serve immediately.

Serves 4

Almond and Apricot Cake

Ingredients

2¹/₂ cups milk

4 tbsp sugar

1 cup arborio rice

3 eggs

3 tbsp candied peel

¹/₂ cup dried apricots,
   chopped

4 tbsp slivered almonds

1 tbsp butter

grated zest of 1 lemon

1 tsp ground cinnamon

1 tsp ground cardamom

confectioners' sugar,
   to decorate

Method

1 Put the milk, sugar, and rice in a saucepan and bring to the boil. Stir, cover, lower the heat, and cook for 15 minutes or until the rice is almost cooked. Cool.

2 Beat the eggs in a bowl and stir in the candied peel, apricots, almonds, butter, lemon zest, cinnamon and cardamom. Stir the rice mixture into this mixture thoroughly.

3 Butter a 8 in/20 cm round cake tin and pour in the combined mixture. Bake in a preheated oven at 350°F/180°C/Gas Mark 4 for 30 minutes or until the top is brown. Dust with the sifted confectioners' sugar.

Serves 6–8

Almond Rice Jelly

Ingredients

3 oz/85 g ground rice

6 oz/170 g ground almonds

2 oz/55 g powdered gelatine

6 oz/170 g superfine sugar

1/4 cup dried coconut

4 1/2 cups boiling water

few drops of almond extract

**canned lychees, gooseberries or
    fresh guava, and cream to serve**

Method

1 Mix together all the dried ingredients. Put into a saucepan, and add the boiling water, while stirring. Bring to the boil. Simmer, still stirring, for 10 minutes until thick. Stir in the almond extract. Pour into lightly greased serving bowl, cool, cover, and refrigerate.

2 Serve with a bowl of canned lychees, gooseberries, or fresh guava, and cream, if desired.

Serves 4

Banana and Raisin Upside-Down Toffee Cake

Ingredients

Topping

3 oz/85 g butter

7 oz/200 g sugar

3½ oz/100 g brown sugar

juice of 1 lemon

2 tbsp boiling water

5 firm bananas

1 cup pecan nuts

1 cup golden raisins

Cake

9 oz/255 g butter

9 oz/255 g brown sugar

4 large eggs

**1 cup buttermilk
   or sour cream**

14 oz/400 g all-purpose flour

2 tsp baking powder

2 tsp ground ginger

2 tsp cinnamon

½ tsp ground nutmeg

clotted cream to serve

Method

1 Grease a 10 in/26 cm springform cake tin and line with a piece of baking paper by placing the paper over the base then replacing and securing the sides of the tin. Set aside.

2 Make the topping first. In a heavy frying pan, melt the butter, then sprinkle both the sugars over the top. Add the lemon juice and boiling water, then bring to the boil. Simmer for 10 minutes until the mixture becomes golden brown and caramelized.

3 Slice the bananas into thick, diagonal pieces and add these to the caramel with the nuts and raisins. Cook over a high heat for 3 minutes to coat the ingredients with the caramel, then spoon this mixture into the prepared cake tin. Smooth gently to cover the entire base of the cake tin and set aside.

4 Beat the butter and sugar together until creamy, then add the eggs one at a time, beating well after each addition. Add the buttermilk or sour cream and combine thoroughly by hand. In a separate bowl, combine the flour, baking powder, ginger, cinnamon, and nutmeg. Add this to the cake batter and mix thoroughly, but gently, by hand.

5 When the batter is well mixed, pour it over the banana topping and smooth the top. Bake at 350°F/180°C/Gas Mark 4 for 75 minutes, or until the surface 'bounces back' when gently pressed in the center.

6 Allow the cake to stand for 5 minutes, then use a plastic spatula to gently separate the cake from the sides of the tin. Place a flat tray (or platter) over the base of the cake and turn over so that the cake is now the right way up. Remove the sides of the tin, then remove the base of the cake tin and gently peel the paper off, leaving behind the succulent toffee banana topping.

7 Serve warm or at room temperature with clotted cream.

Serves 8

Banana and Coconut Cake

Ingredients

4 oz/115 g butter, at
   room temperature
1 cup superfine sugar
2 eggs
3 ripe bananas
1/2 cup lemon juice
1 1/2 cups all-purpose flour
1 1/2 tsp baking powder
1/2 tsp ground cinnamon
1 cup dried coconut
cream or ice cream and
   fruit to serve

Method

1 Preheat oven to 350°F/180°C/Gas Mark 4. Lightly grease a 20 cm/8 in cake tin and line the bottom with baking paper.

2 Combine the butter and sugar in a mixing bowl. Cream together until light and fluffy. Add the eggs, 1 at a time, and beat well after each addition.

3 Place the bananas in a food processor with the lemon juice. Process until very mushy. Stir the bananas through the mixture. Add the flour, soda, cinnamon, and coconut. Stir until combined.

4 Spoon the mixture into the prepared cake tin and bake in preheated oven for 40–45 minutes or until cooked. Leave the cake to cool for 10–15 minutes, then turn out onto a cake rack.

5 Cut into wedges and serve with cream or ice cream and fruit.

Serves 6–8

Banana Mousse

Ingredients

1 tbsp gelatine

¼ cup boiling water

1 lb/455 g ripe bananas

¼ cup sugar

1 tbsp lemon juice

1 cup thickened heavy cream

3½ fl oz/100 mL coconut milk

**3½ oz/100 g bittersweet
  chocolate, melted**

Method

1 Place the gelatine and boiling water in a bowl and stir until the gelatine dissolves. Set aside to cool.

2 Place the bananas, sugar, and lemon juice in a food processor and process until smooth. Stir the gelatine mixture into the banana mixture.

3 Place the cream and coconut milk in a bowl and beat until soft peaks form. Fold the cream mixture into banana mixture.

4 Spoon the mousse into 6 serving glasses or a loaf tin.

5 Divide the melted chocolate between the glasses or drizzle over the mixture in the loaf tin and swirl with a skewer. Refrigerate for 2 hours or until set.

Note: When available, dried banana chips make an attractive garnish with fresh mint leaves.

Serves 6

The Best Mud Cake

Ingredients

**12 oz/340 g bittersweet chocolate,
  broken into pieces**

³/₄ cup superfine sugar

6 oz/170 g butter, chopped

5 eggs, separated

¹/₃ cup all-purpose flour, sifted

cocoa powder, sifted

confectioners' sugar, sifted

Method

1   Place the chocolate, superfine sugar, and butter in a heatproof bowl set over a saucepan of simmering water and heat, stirring, until the mixture is smooth. Remove the bowl and set aside to cool slightly. Beat in the egg yolks 1 at a time, beating well after each addition. Fold in the flour.

2   Place the egg whites in a clean bowl and beat until stiff peaks form. Fold the egg whites into the chocolate mixture. Pour the mixture into a greased 9 in/23 cm springform tin and bake at 350°F/180°C/Gas Mark 4 for 45 minutes or until cake is cooked when tested with a skewer. Cool the cake in tin.

3   Just prior to serving, dust the cake with the cocoa powder and confectioners' sugar.

Serves 8–10

Black and White Tart

Ingredients

Macaroon Shell

2 egg whites

¹/₂ cup superfine sugar

7 oz/200 g dried coconut

¹/₄ cup all-purpose flour, sifted

Chocolate Sour Cream Filling

2 egg yolks

³/₄ cup thickened heavy cream

6 oz/170 g bittersweet chocolate

2 tbsp cognac or brandy

6 oz/170 g white chocolate

²/₃ cup sour cream

Raspberry Coulis

1 cup raspberries

1 tbsp confectioners' sugar

Method

1 Place the egg whites in a bowl and beat until soft peaks form. Gradually beat in the superfine sugar. Fold in the coconut and flour. Press the mixture over base and up sides of a greased and lined 23 cm/9 in round flan tin with a removable base. Bake at 350°/180°C/Gas Mark 4 for 20–25 minutes or until golden. Stand in the tin for 5 minutes then remove and place on a wire rack to cool.

2 To make the filling, place the egg yolks and cream in a heatproof bowl set over a saucepan of simmering water and beat until thick and pale. Stir in the bittersweet chocolate and cognac or brandy and continue stirring until the chocolate melts. Remove the bowl from the pan and set aside to cool.

3 Place the white chocolate and sour cream in a heatproof bowl set over a saucepan of simmering water and heat, stirring, until the mixture is smooth. Remove the bowl from the pan and set aside to cool.

4 Place alternating spoonfuls of the dark and white mixtures in the macaroon shell and, using a skewer, swirl the mixtures to give a marbled effect. Chill for 2 hours or until the filling is firm.

5 To make the coulis, place the raspberries in a food processor or blender and process to make a purée. Press the purée through a sieve to remove the seeds, then stir in the confectioners' sugar. Serve with the tart.

Note: This dessert is best served the day it is made as the macaroon shell may absorb too much moisture on standing and lose its crispness.

Serves 8

Caramel Custard

Ingredients

¹/₂ **cup plus 6 tbsp sugar**

2 tbsp water

3 whole eggs

2 egg yolks

2¹/₂ cups milk

¹/₈ **tsp salt**

¹/₄ **tsp grated lemon zest**

whipped cream, optional

Method

1 To caramelize the sugar, in a small heavy saucepan, heat ¹/₂ cup of the sugar with the water over a medium heat, stirring constantly, until the syrup turns golden in color (the sugar will crystallize before it liquifies). Immediately pour the syrup into 6 individual custard cups.

2 Preheat the oven to 350°F/180°C/Gas Mark 4. Whisk whole eggs and egg yolks in a large bowl until uniform in color. Whisk in the milk, remaining sugar, salt and lemon zest. Divide the mixture among the prepared cups. Place the cups in a baking pan and add enough hot water to come halfway up the sides of the cups. Bake for about 45 minutes, or until a knife inserted in the custard comes out clean. Remove the cups from the pan and allow to cool. Cover and refrigerate until chilled.

3 Run a knife around the edge of each cup and unmould the flan, spooning the caramelized sugar over it. Serve with the whipped cream, if desired.

Serves 6

Cassata Alla Siciliana

Ingredients

4 eggs

¹/₂ cup superfine sugar

³/₄ cup all-purpose flour, sifted

³/₄ tsp baking powder

¹/₃ cup brandy

Cassata Filling

¹/₂ cup sugar

4 tsp water

13 oz/370 g ricotta cheese

¹/₂ cup thickened heavy cream, whipped

¹/₄ cup candied, chopped

3¹/₂ oz/100 g dark bittersweet, finely chopped

¹/₄ cup candied cherries, quartered

1¹/₂ oz/45 g unsalted pistachio nuts, chopped

Chocolate Topping

11 oz/310 g bittersweet chocolate

3 oz/85 g butter

Method

1 Place the eggs in a large mixing bowl and beat until light and fluffy. Gradually add the sugar, beating well after each addition until the mixture is creamy. Fold in the flour. Pour the batter into a greased and lined 26 × 10¹/₂ in/32 cm ×12³/₄ in Swiss roll-tin and bake for 10–12 minutes or until cooked when tested with a skewer. Turn onto a wire rack to cool.

2 To make the filling, place the sugar and water in a saucepan and cook over a low heat, stirring constantly, until the sugar dissolves. Remove from the heat and set aside to cool. Place the ricotta cheese in a food processor or blender and process until smooth. Transfer to a bowl and mix in the sugar syrup, cream, candied peel, chocolate, cherries, and nuts.

3 Line an 11 × 4¹/₂ in/21 cm × 8¹/₂ in loaf dish with plastic wrap. Cut the cake into slices and sprinkle with the brandy. Line the base and sides of prepared dish with the cake. Spoon the filling into the loaf dish and top with a final layer of cake. Cover and freeze until solid.

4 To make the chocolate topping, place the chocolate and butter in a saucepan and cook, stirring, over a low heat until melted and the mixture is well blended. Allow to cool slightly.

5 Turn the cassata onto a wire rack and cover with topping. Return to the freezer until the chocolate sets.

Note: Decorate with candied fruits and serve with whipped cream.

Serves 10

Champagne Sherbet

Ingredients

1¹/₂ cups water

7 oz/200 g granulated sugar

grated zest of 2 lemons

juice of 2 lemons

1¹/₄ cups whipping cream

1¹/₄ cups plain yogurt

¹/₄ bottle sweet champagne

1 egg white

sponge fingers or wafers
  to serve

Method

1 Place the water, and sugar with the lemon rind in a saucepan and simmer for 10 minutes. Cool and combine with the lemon juice. Lightly whip the cream, fold in yogurt, and strain in the cooled lemon juice and syrup.

2 Pour into a container and freeze until mushy. Remove from the freezer, beat well, and then add the champagne. Freeze again to the mushy stage. Beat again and fold in the stiffly beaten egg white. Freeze until firm and serve with a sponge finger or wafers.

Serves 8

Devil's Food Cake

Ingredients

1 cup cocoa powder

1¹/₂ cups boiling water

13 oz/370 g sweet butter, softened

1 tsp vanilla extract

1¹/₂ cups superfine sugar

4 eggs

2¹/₂ cups flour

¹/₂ cup cornstarch

1 tsp baking soda

1 tsp salt

**¹/₂ cup thickened
   heavy cream, whipped**

Chocolate Butter Icing

8 oz/225 g butter, softened

1 egg and 2 egg yolks

1 cup confectioners' sugar, sifted

**6 oz/170 g bittersweet chocolate,
   melted and cooled**

Method

1 Combine the cocoa powder and water in a small bowl and mix until blended. Set aside to cool. Place the butter and vanilla extract in a large mixing bowl and beat until light and fluffy. Gradually add the sugar, beating well after each addition until the mixture is creamy. Beat in the eggs one at a time, beating well after each addition.

2 Sift together the flour, cornstarch, baking soda, and salt into a bowl. Fold the flour mixture and cocoa mixture alternately into the egg mixture.

3 Divide the batter between 3 greased and lined 9 in/23 cm sandwich tins and bake at 350°F/180°C/Gas Mark 4 for 20–25 minutes or until the cakes are cooked when tested with a skewer. Stand in the tins for 5 minutes before turning onto wire racks to cool completely.

4 To make the icing, place the butter in a mixing bowl and beat until light and fluffy. Mix in the egg, egg yolks, and confectioners' sugar. Add the chocolate and beat until the icing is thick and creamy. Sandwich the cakes together using the whipped cream, then cover the top and sides with the icing.

Serves 12

Double-Fudge Blondies

Ingredients

8 oz/225 g butter, softened

1½ cups sugar

1 tsp vanilla extract

4 eggs, lightly beaten

1½ cups flour

½ tsp baking powder

6 oz/170 g white chocolate, melted

Cream-Cheese Filling

8 oz/225 g cream cheese, softened

2 oz/55 g white chocolate, melted

¼ cup maple syrup

1 egg

1 tbsp all-purpose flour

confectioners' sugar to serve

Method

1 To make the filling, place the cream cheese, chocolate, maple syrup, egg, and flour in a bowl and beat until smooth. Set aside.

2 Place the butter, sugar, and vanilla extract in a bowl and beat until light and fluffy. Gradually beat in the eggs.

3 Sift together the flour and baking powder over the butter mixture. Add the chocolate and mix well to combine.

4 Spread ½ the mixture over the base of a greased and lined 9 in/23 cm square cake tin. Top with the cream-cheese filling, and then with the remaining mixture. Bake at 350°F/180°C/Gas Mark 4 for 40 minutes or until firm. Cool in tin, then cut into squares. To serve, dust with the confectioners' sugar.

Note: These lusciously rich white brownies can double as a dinner party dessert if drizzled with melted white or bittersweet chocolate and topped with toasted flaked almonds.

Makes 24

Fruit Salad in Lime Spicy Syrup

Ingredients

½ pineapple, diced

1 mango, diced

1 papaya, diced

1 apple, cored and diced

1 cucumber, diced

12 rambutans, peeled and deseeded

Syrup

1 cup grated palm sugar or brown sugar

⅓ cup water

rind of 1 lime

2 tbsp lime juice

1 tsp tamarind concentrate

1 medium chili, deseeded
   and finely chopped

Method

1   Combine the sugar, water, lime rind, and lime juice in a small saucepan. Bring to the boil and simmer over a low heat for 8–10 minutes and allow to cool. Add the tamarind and chili and stir to combine.

2   Combine the fruit in a serving bowl. Pour over the syrup and toss.

Serves 4

Fruit-Filled Chimichangas

Ingredients

4 flour tortillas

vegetable oil for deep-frying

sugar for sprinkling

cream or ice cream to serve

Fruit and Coconut Filling

¹/₂ cup chopped pineapple

¹/₄ cup chopped strawberries

4 tbsp flaked coconut

2 tbsp chopped fresh mint

Method

1 To make the filling, place the pineapple, strawberries, coconut, and mint in a bowl and mix to combine.

2 Warm the tortillas, 1 at a time, in a dry-frying pan over a medium heat for 20–30 seconds on each side or until soft. Place 1–2 tablespoons of the filling down the center of each tortilla and fold in ¹/₂ to enclose. Press the edges together to seal.

3 Heat the oil in a saucepan over a high heat until a cube of bread dropped in browns in 50 seconds. Hold the tortilla parcels with 2 sets of tongs and carefully deep-fry for 2–3 minutes or until golden and crisp. Drain on absorbent kitchen paper, then sprinkle generously the with sugar and serve with cream or ice cream.

Serves 4

Ginger Cake

Ingredients

5 oz/145 g butter

4 oz/115 g dark brown sugar

2 eggs

8 oz/225 g all-purpose flour

2 tsp ground ginger

1 tsp salt

11 oz/315 g corn syrup

¹/₂ cup raisins

¹/₂ tsp baking soda

**¹/₂ cup confectioners' sugar to
serve milk, warmed**

Method

1 Beat the butter until it is light and fluffy. Add the sugar and beat until light. Beat in the eggs, 1 at a time. Fold in the flour, ginger, and salt. Then stir in the corn syrup and raisins. Add the baking of soda to the milk and gently stir it into the cake mixture.

2 Grease a 8 in/20 cm. cake tin. Pour the mixture in and place in oven preheated to350°F/180°C/Gas Mark 4. Bake for 1¹/₂ hours. If the top is getting too brown, turn the oven down for the last 30 minutes. Remove from the oven. After 10 minutes, turn the cake out onto a rack. Cool, then dust with confectioners' sugar.

Serves 10–12

Ginger Melon Soup

Ingredients

1 cantaloupe melon (about 1²/₃ lb/750 g)
2 oz/55 g ginger, peeled
3¹/₂ cups water
¹/₂ cup sugar
11 oz/315 g glass noodles
juice of 2 limes or lemons
4 sprigs of mint leaves to garnish

Method

1 Peel the melon, remove the seeds, cut into small cubes, and blend or process. Keep cool. Slice the ginger finely and boil ¹/₂ of it in water with ¹/₂ the sugar until dissolved. Turn the heat down, and add the noodles to simmer for 5 minutes. Remove from the heat, allow to cool, and pour into a bowl. Remove the ginger and chill.

2 In a saucepan, boil together the remaining sugar, ginger, and lime or lemon juice. Simmer until thick. Remove from the heat, cool, and remove the ginger. Chill.

3 In individual bowls set in larger ice-filled bowls, pour equal quantities of the gingered melon purée. Top with the noodles, then the lime or lemon mix. Garnish each with a mint leaf and serve with ginger biscuits to dunk and soften.

Serves 4

Gulub Jamun

Ingredients

6 oz/170 g sugar

2¹/₂ cups water

8 green cardamom pods

1 oz/30 g all-purpose flour

**4 oz/115 g powdered
   skimmed milk**

1 oz/30 g ghee or butter

1 oz/30 g cream cheese

1–2 tbsp rosewater

**2–3 tbsp milk or
   plain low-fat yogurt,**

oil for deep-frying

Method

1 Put 5 oz/145 g of the sugar with the measured water in a wide saucepan or deep-frying pan. Stir over a gentle heat until the sugar has dissolved, then add the cardamom pods. Increase the heat and boil for 15 minutes to make a light syrup. Reduce the heat to the lowest setting to keep the syrup warm.

2 Combine the flour and powdered milk in a bowl. Rub in the ghee or butter, then add the remaining sugar, cream cheese, rosewater and enough milk or yogurt to form a soft dough. Knead lightly and roll into 18 small balls.

3 Heat the oil for deep-frying. Cook the jamuns in small batches, keeping them moving in the oil until they are golden brown all over.

4 When golden brown, remove the jamuns with a slotted spoon and drain on paper towels for 5 minutes. Remove the syrup from the heat and carefully add the jamuns. Allow to cool to room temperature in the syrup. To serve, transfer jamuns to individual plates with a slotted spoon, then add 2–3 tablespoons of the syrup.

Note: These small dumplings in a spicy syrup are a traditional dessert. They are usually made with full-fat powdered milk. This is not always easy to obtain, so this recipe uses skimmed milk powder and adds cream cheese.

Serves 6

Frangelico Chocolate Cake with Raspberry Sauce

Ingredients

7 oz/200 g bittersweet chocolate, chopped

3¹/₂ oz/100 g butter

5 eggs, separated

¹/₂ cup superfine sugar

¹/₃ cup all-purpose flour

¹/₃ tsp baking powder sifted

¹/₂ cup hazelnuts, ground

1¹/₂ fl oz/45mL frangelico liqueur

Raspberry Sauce

4 oz/225 g raspberries

2 tbsp confectioners' sugar

1 tbsp lemon juice

Method

1 Preheat the oven to 370°F/190°C/Gas Mark 5.

2 Melt the chocolate and butter over hot water, remove from the heat, and stir in the egg yolks, sugar, flour, hazelnuts, and Frangelico.

3 Beat the egg whites until soft peaks form. Fold lightly into the chocolate mixture and pour into a greased and lined round 8 in/20 cm cake tin and bake for 40–45 minutes, or until the cake shrinks slightly from the sides of the tin.

4 To make the raspberry sauce, place the raspberries, confectioners' sugar, and lemon juice in a food processor, and blend, until smooth. Strain, and add a little water if the mixture is too thick.

5 Serve the cake, cut into wedges, with the raspberry. You can dust the cake with extra confectioners' sugar, if you wish.

Serves 8

Lemon Polenta Cake with Raspberry Filling

Ingredients

Filling

**2 cups raspberries,
    fresh or frozen**

2 tbsp sugar

1 tbsp cornstarch

Cake

7 oz/200 g butter, softened

³/₄ cup sugar

juice and zest from 2 lemons

3 large eggs

1¹/₄ cups all-purpose flour

1 cup cornstarch

2 tsp baking powder

¹/₄ tsp salt

¹/₂ cup polenta

2 tbsp superfine sugar

³/₄ cup sliced almonds, toasted

1–2 containers fresh raspberries

confectioners' sugar, for dusting

heavy cream (to serve)

Method

1 First, make the filling. Purée the raspberries in a processor with the sugar and cornstarch and process until smooth. Transfer the mixture to a small saucepan and bring to the boil. Stir over a medium heat until the mixture boils and thickens (about 3 minutes). Cool completely.

2 Next, make the cake. Preheat the oven to 350°F/180°C/Gas Mark 4 and lightly butter a 9¹/₂ in/24 cm-springform cake tin. Add a little flour to the tin to dust lightly, then shake out the excess.

3 Using an electric mixer, beat the butter, sugar, and lemon zest in large bowl until fluffy. Add the eggs 1 at a time, beating well after each addition. Sift the flour, cornstarch, baking powder, and salt into a medium bowl, then add the polenta. Add the dry mixture to the butter and egg mixture with the lemon juice and stir until well combined—do not over-mix.

4 Transfer the batter to the prepared pan. Sprinkle the sugar and toasted almonds over the cake evenly, then bake for 40 minutes or until the cake is golden, and a toothpick inserted into center comes out with a few moist crumbs attached.

5 Transfer the cake to a wire rack and allow to cool for 20 minutes. Turn the cake out and cool completely.

6 When the cake is cold, slice in half so that you have 2 layers. Place the first layer on a cake plate and top with the raspberry filling and most of the fresh raspberries. Add the top layer (the 1 with the almond-sugar coating) and press gently.

7 Dust with the confectioners' sugar, top with the remaining fresh raspberries, and serve with the heavy cream.

Serves 8–10

Muddy Mud Cake

Ingredients

9 oz/255 g butter

9 oz/255 g bittersweet or semi-sweet chocolate, chopped

3½ oz/100 g superfine sugar

3 oz/85 g brown sugar

1 tbsp brandy

1½ cups hot water

¾ cup all-purpose flour

¾ tsp baking powder

3 tablespoons Dutch cocoa

2 eggs

1 tsp vanilla extract

confectioners' sugar, for dusting

cream or ice cream, to serve

Method

1 Preheat the oven to 300°F/150°C/Gas Mark 2 and butter a 9½ in/24 cm non-stick springform cake tin, or small molds.

2 In a saucepan, melt the butter, then add the chopped chocolate, superfine and brown sugars, brandy and hot water. Mix well with a whisk until the mixture is smooth.

3 Mix the flour and cocoa and add to the chocolate mixture with the eggs and vanilla. Beat just until combined. (Do not worry if the mixture is lumpy.)

4 Pour into the prepared cake tin and bake in the preheated oven for 50 minutes or the molds for 30 minutes. Allow to cool in the tin for 15 minutes, then turn out.

5 To serve, dust with the confectioners' sugar and serve warm with cream or ice cream.

Note: You can serve the cake cut into individual-sized squares that are split in 2 and filled with vanilla ice cream and coated with hot fudge sauce, to turn this recipe into a hot brownie sundae. You could also serve the individual cakes with hot fudge sauce.

Serves 4

Orange Cardamom Cakes

Ingredients

Cakes

2 cups all-purpose flour

1½ tsp baking powder

1 tsp baking soda

2 tsp ground cardamom

½ cup butter, softened

1 cup sugar

zest and juice of 2 oranges

2 large eggs

⅔ cup yogurt

3 tbsp marmalade

2 tbsp boiling water

2 tbsp sugar, extra

Orange Sauce

2 cups sugar

1 cup water

juice of two oranges

2 tbsp heavy cream

4 large oranges, segmented

Method

1 Preheat the oven to 350°F/180°C/Gas Mark 4 and generously butter 2 non-stick 'Texas' muffin pans each with 6 cavities.

2 In a large bowl, combine the flour, baking powder, baking soda, and ground cardamom. Set aside.

3 Using an electric mixer, cream the butter, sugar, and orange zest together until light and fluffy. Add the eggs and yogurt and mix on low speed until the ingredients are well combined, then fold the flour mixture in by hand – do not over-mix.

4 Divide the batter evenly among the 10–12 muffin cups and bake at for 15–18 minutes, approximately. Meanwhile, whisk together the fresh orange juice, marmalade, boiling water and extra 2 tablespoons sugar.

5 When the orange cakes are ready to come out of the oven, remove the muffin tins, then spoon the orange syrup over the cakes and allow them to cool in the tins.

6 Meanwhile, make the sauce. Mix together the sugar and water and stir until the sugar has dissolved. Raise the heat and boil vigorously, washing down the sides of the pan with a pastry brush dipped in cold water. Continue boiling until the syrup turns a rich, deep gold, then remove the pan from the heat. Carefully add the orange juice to the syrup (be careful because it will splatter). Swirl the pan to dissolve the juice, returning the pan to the heat if necessary. Once the mixture is smooth, remove from the heat and set aside to cool. When cool, whisk in the cream, then chill the sauce.

7 To serve, turn out the cakes and place each on a plate, heap the orange segments on top of the cakes, then spoon the sauce all around.

Serves 10–12

Passionfruit Zabaglione with Fresh Berries

Ingredients

5 egg yolks

½ cup superfine sugar

½ cup sweet white wine

¼ cup passionfruit pulp

4 oz/115 g blueberries

5 oz/145 g raspberries

5 oz/145 g strawberries

Method

1 Combine the egg yolks and sugar in a heatproof bowl, and beat, until thick and pale. Beat through the sweet wine, and place the bowl over a saucepan of simmering water. Continue to beat for 15 minutes, or until the mixture is very thick, not allowing the bowl to overheat too much. The mixture is ready when it forms soft mounds.

2 Remove the bowl from the heat, and continue beating for a further 5 minutes, or until the mixture has cooled. Fold through the passionfruit pulp, and serve with the fresh berries.

3 For Vanilla Zabaglione, omit the passionfruit pulp and add the seeds from 1 vanilla pod by splitting the pod down the middle and scraping out the seeds.

Serves 4–6

Passionfruit Souffle

Ingredients

2 oz/55 g ricotta cheese

1½ cups passionfruit pulp

2 egg yolks

1 tbsp orange-flavored liqueur

½ cup superfine sugar

6 egg whites

pinch cream of tartar

confectioners' sugar, sifted

Method

1 Place the ricotta cheese, passionfruit pulp, egg yolks, liqueur, and ½ the superfine sugar in a bowl and beat for 5 minutes or until the mixture is smooth.

2 Place the egg whites and cream of tartar in a clean bowl and beat until soft peaks form. Gradually beat in the remaining superfine sugar until stiff peaks form.

3 Fold ⅓ of the egg white mixture into the passionfruit mixture, then fold in the remaining egg white mixture.

4 Pour the soufflé mixture into a greased 8 in/20 cm soufflé dish and bake for 20 minutes or until soufflé is well risen. Sprinkle with the confectioners' sugar and serve.

Serves 4–6

Poppyseed Cheesecake

Ingredients

Filling

1 cup poppyseeds

1 lb/455 g cream cheese

1 lb/455 g ricotta cheese

½ cup sugar

6 eggs

14 oz/400 g can sweetened condensed milk

1 tbsp vanilla essence

1 cup lemon curd (see below)

Lemon Curd

3 lemons, zest grated and juice strained

2½ oz/75 g butter

9 oz/255 g sugar

3 large eggs or 8 yolks, for a richer curd

Method

1 Preheat the oven to 400°F/200°C/Gas Mark 6 and generously butter a 4½ in/24 cm non-stick cake tin.

2 Sprinkle about ½ the poppyseeds over the base and sides of the cake tin, then tip out the excess and reserve with the remaining poppyseeds.

3 Beat the cream cheese and the ricotta in an electric mixer until very smooth, then add the sugar and continue for 2 minutes. Add the eggs, 1 at a time and beating well after each addition, then finally, add the sweetened milk and vanilla and beat for 1 more minute. Using a spatula, stir around the sides if necessary. Add the poppyseeds and mix well to distribute them throughout the cheese mixture.

4 Pour the mixture into the prepared tin and smooth the top gently by tapping the tin on the counter. Bake for 10 minutes, then reduce the heat to 350°F/160°C/Gas Mark 3 and cook for a further 40 minutes, or until the mixture is still slightly 'wobbly'.

5 Allow the cake to cool in the tin, undisturbed, until cold. When the cake is cold, carefully smooth the lemon curd over the surface of the cake, then sprinkle the remaining poppyseeds over the entire surface. When the curd is set, remove the side of the tin and serve.

6 To make the lemon curd, place the lemon rind, juice, butter, and sugar in the top of a double boiler or in a heatproof bowl over a saucepan of simmering water. Heat, stirring until the sugar dissolves and the mixture is quite warm. Add the eggs and mix very well with a whisk to distribute them thoroughly, and continue stirring while the mixture heats. Keep stirring until the mixture coats the back of a spoon, which indicates that the eggs have thickened and set. Do not allow the mixture to boil because the eggs will curdle. Allow to cool a little, then spread over the cake.

Note: This cake can be made up to three days ahead.

Serves 10–12

Raspberry Mousse

Ingredients

1 lb/455 g fresh or frozen raspberries

**2 tsp gelatine dissolved in
    2 tbsp hot water, cooled**

**4 oz/115 g ricotta or curd
    cheese, drained**

4 eggs, separated

¼ cup superfine sugar

whipped cream

chocolate curls, to garnish, optional

Method

1 Place the raspberries in a food processor or blender and process to make a purée. Push the purée through a sieve to remove the seeds and set aside. Stir the gelatine mixture into the purée and set aside.

2 Place the ricotta or curd cheese in a food processor or blender and process until smooth. Set aside.

3 Place the egg yolks and sugar in a heatproof bowl, set over a saucepan of simmering water and beat until a ribbon trail forms when the beater is lifted from the mixture. Remove bowl from heat. Whisk the egg yolk mixture, then the ricotta or curd cheese into the raspberry purée. Cover and chill until just beginning to set.

4 Place the egg whites in a bowl and beat until stiff peaks form. Fold the egg white mixture into the fruit mixture. Spoon the mousse mixture into 4 lightly oiled ½ cup capacity molds or ramekins, cover, and chill until set.

5 To serve, garnish with the chocolate curls, if desired.

Serves 4

Ricotta Cheesecake

Ingredients

Pastry
8 oz/225 g all-purpose flour
4 oz/115 g butter
1 egg yolk, beaten

Filling
1½ lb/680 g ricotta cheese
4 oz/115 g superfine sugar
2 oz/55 g ground almonds
grated rind of 1 lemon
½ tsp vanilla extract
4 eggs

Method

1 To make the pastry, sift the flour into a bowl and rub in the butter until the mixture resembles fine breadcrumbs. Add the egg yolk and enough iced water to make a firm dough. Chill for 1 hour. Roll out the dough and use it to line a greased 9 in/23 cm pie dish or springform tin. Chill for 1 hour.

2 To make the filling, combine the ricotta, sugar, almonds, and lemon rind. Beat in the vanilla and eggs, 1 at a time. Pour into the chilled pastry case and bake in a preheated very hot oven at 430°F/220°C/Gas Mark 7 for 5 minutes, then reduce the heat to moderate 350°F/180°C/Gas Mark 4 and bake for a further 30 minutes or until the center of the filling is firm. Cool and chill.

Note: This cheesecake is surprisingly easy to make, so don't be deterred if the instructions look complicated.

Serves 8

Mango Ice Cream

Ingredients

8 egg yolks

1¼ cups superfine sugar

4 cups milk

2 cups heavy cream

2 tsp vanilla essence

1 cup mango, puréed

Method

1 Place the egg yolks and sugar in a mixing bowl and beat until thick and creamy.

2 Place the milk and cream in a large saucepan and bring just to the boil. Remove from the heat and whisk gradually into the egg yolk mixture. Return to the pan and cook over a low heat, stirring constantly, until the mixture coats the back of a wooden spoon.

3 Stir in the vanilla essence and fold in the mango purée. Transfer the mixture to an ice cream maker and freeze according to the manufacturer's instructions.

Note: If you do not have an ice cream maker, place the custard mixture in a deep-sided metal container and freeze until the mixture begins to set around the edge. Then remove from freezer and beat with an electric mixer until smooth. To ensure a smooth texture, repeat this process 2–3 times more to prevent large ice crystals forming.

Makes 5 cups

Lemon, and Yogurt Semolina Cake

Ingredients

4 oz/115 g butter, softened

³/₄ cup superfine sugar

zest from 1 lemon, finely grated

4 eggs

1 cup fine semolina

2 tsp baking powder

1 cup ground almond

1 cup golden raisins

¹/₂ cup almonds, flaked

7 oz/200 g yogurt

cream to serve

Syrup

1 cup superfine sugar

¹/₂ cup lemon juice

¹/₂ cup honey

Method

1 Preheat the oven to 350°F/180°C/Gas Mark 4.

2 Grease a 8 in/20 cm cake tin, and line with paper.

3 In a large bowl, add the butter, sugar, and rind. Using an electric beater, cream until light and soft. Add the eggs 1 at a time, and beat well after each egg.

4 Fold in the semolina, baking powder, and ground almond. Add the golden raisins, almonds, and yogurt, and lightly fold in.

5 Pour the mixture into the prepared cake tin and bake for 35–45 minutes or until the cake is lightly browned on top.

6 To make the syrup in a small saucepan, combine the sugar, lemon juice, and honey. Cook on a low heat for 15–20 minutes or until it forms a syrup.

7 Using a skewer, poke the cake evenly. Cool the syrup slightly, and pour over the cake. Serve with the cream.

Serves 6–8

Fruit with Passionfruit Custard

Ingredients

2 quinces, peeled
¹/₂ cup sugar
¹/₄ cup sweet dessert wine
water

Passionfruit Custard
³/₄ cup milk
I tsp vanilla extract
2 egg yolks
¹/₃ cup passionfruit pulp
¹/₂ cup heavy cream, whipped

Method

1 Place the quinces in a large saucepan. Add the sugar, wine, and enough water to cover. Bring to the boil, then reduce the heat and simmer for 3 hours or until the quinces are tender and a rich pink color.

2 To make the custard, place the milk and vanilla extract in a saucepan and heat over a medium heat until almost boiling. Whisk in the egg yolks and cook, stirring, until the mixture thickens. Remove the pan from the heat and set aside to cool. Fold the passionfruit pulp and cream into the custard.

3 To serve, cut the quinces into ¹/₄ and serve with the custard.

Note: When quinces are unavailable, peaches, nectarines, or pears are all delicious alternatives. Just remember most other fruit will only require 15–30 minutes cooking. The Passionfruit Custard is delicious served with almost any poached fruit. If fresh passionfruit is not available, canned passionfruit pulp may be used instead.

Serves 4

Fruit Salad with Lemon and Ginger Syrup

Ingredients

3 nectarines, stoned and sliced

**8 oz/225 g punnet strawberries,
   sliced**

**3 clementines, peeled and
   segmented**

**¹/₂ cantaloupe or charentais melon,
   deseeded and sliced**

extra heavy cream, to serve, optional

Syrup

¹/₂ cup golden sugar

juice of 2 lemons

**4 in/10 cm piece fresh root ginger,
   grated**

Method

1 To make the syrup, place the sugar in a small, heavy-based saucepan, add the lemon juice and ginger, and gently heat, until the sugar is dissolved. Bring to the boil, then simmer for 2 minutes. Strain through a sieve, discarding the ginger.

2 Place the prepared fruits in individual glass bowls or a large glass bowl and pour over the warm syrup. Toss gently and chill for up to 2 hours. Serve with some extra heavy cream, if wished.

Serves 4

Glazed Fruit in Hazelnut Filo Baskets

Ingredients

2 tbsp roasted ground, unsalted hazelnuts or other unsalted nuts of your choice

1 tsp ground cinnamon

2 tsp sugar

6 sheets filo pastry

unsaturated oil or melted unsaturated margarine for brushing pastry

1/2 cup prepared blackcurrant jelly or flavor of your choice

3 cups chopped mixed fresh seasonal fruit (blueberries, paya, kiwi fruit, peaches, raspberries, strawberries, mango, pineapple, passionfruit, and melon)

confectioners' sugar

Custard Cream

1/2 cup low-fat custard

1/2 cup reduced-fat fresh ricotta cheese

1/4 cup evaporated skim milk

1 tsp vanilla extract

Method

1 To make the custard cream, place the custard, ricotta cheese, evaporated milk, and vanilla extract in a blender. Process until smooth. Pour into a bowl. Cover. Refrigerate until ready to serve.

2 Preheat the oven to 330°F/170°C/Gas Mark 3. Lightly spray or brush 4 x 1 cup capacity ramekins with unsaturated oil. You can do this on the outside or inside of the ramekins, depending on whether you want to drape the pastry over the upturned 'mold' or lay it inside the dish as you would a pie. Be guided by the size and shape of the basket you want to end up with. Place the dishes on a baking tray.

3 Place the ground nuts, cinnamon, and sugar in a small bowl. Mix to combine. Lay 2 sheets of filo pastry on a clean, dry surface. Lightly spray or brush with the unsaturated oil. Sprinkle with 1/2 the nut mixture. Lay another 2 sheets of pastry on top. Repeat with the oil and nut mixture. Top with the remaining sheets of pastry. Cut the stack into 1/4. Arrange the pastry in or over the dishes as described above. Bake for 10–15 minutes or until golden.

4 Just before serving, place the jelly in a saucepan over a low heat. Melt. Add the fruit, and toss to combine.

5 To serve, place a basket on each serving plate. Divide the fruit mixture between the baskets. Sprinkle with the confectioners' sugar and accompany with the custard cream.

Makes 4 baskets

Layered Fruit Mold

Ingredients

1 cup low-fat vanilla frûche

¹/₂ cup reduced-fat fresh ricotta cheese

3 tsp gelatine

2 tbsp hot water

3 oz/85 g packet port wine or other
   jelly crystals of your choice

3 cups berries or fruit of choice
   except for fresh pineapple,
   kiwi fruit, or paya

Method

1 Place the frûche and ricotta cheese in a food processor. Process until smooth. Dissolve the gelatine in the hot water, and stir into the frûche mixture.

2 Rinse 8 x 1 cup capacity moulds or glasses with cold water. Divide the frûche mixture between the molds. Chill until set.

3 Prepare the jelly according to the packet directions. Cool. Arrange the fruit on top of the set frûche mixture. Carefully pour over the cooled jelly. Chill until set.

4 To serve, quickly dip the molds into a basin of hot water. Turn onto serving plates. Alternatively, serve straight from the glasses.

Serves 8

Lemon and Ginger Syllabub

Ingredients

10 fl oz/285 mL carton heavy cream

**⅓ cup ginger wine or medium
   sweet white wine**

**finely grated rind and juice of 1 large
   lemon**

¼ cup superfine sugar

**2 pieces preserved ginger in syrup,
   drained**

fresh mint to decorate

Method

1 Whip the cream until slightly thickened. Gradually whisk in the ginger wine or white wine, lemon rind and juice, and the sugar.

2 Slice 1 piece of the preserved ginger into matchsticks and set aside. Finely chop the remaining piece, then fold into the cream mixture.

3 Spoon the mixture into small glasses or bowls and refrigerate for 30 minutes. Decorate with the reserved preserved ginger matchsticks and the mint.

Serves 4

Lemon Ricotta Cheesecake

Ingredients

2 oz/55 g butter

3¹/₂ oz/100 g digestive cookies, ground

1¹/₂ oz/45 g ground almonds

3 lemons

9 oz/255 g tub ricotta

5 oz/145 g plain yogurt

3 eggs

1 tbsp cornstarch

3 oz/85 g superfine sugar

1 tbsp clear honey

Method

1 Preheat the oven to 350°F/180°C/Gas Mark 4. Melt the butter in a saucepan, then stir in the cookies and almonds. Press into the base of a deep, lightly greased 8 in/20 cm loose-bottomed cake tin. Cook in the oven for 10 minutes.

2 Meanwhile, finely grate the rind from 2 of the lemons and squeeze the juice. Blend with the ricotta, yogurt, eggs, cornstarch, and sugar in a food processor until smooth, or beat with a hand whisk. Pour the mixture over the cookie base and bake for 45–50 minutes, until lightly set and golden. Cool in the tin for at least 1 hour, then run a knife around the edge to loosen and turn out onto a serving plate.

3 Thinly slice the remaining lemon. Place in a saucepan, cover with boiling water and simmer for 5 minutes, then drain. Heat the honey over a low heat, but do not let it boil. Dip the lemon slices in the honey and arrange over the cheesecake.

Serves 6

Mango Oat Crunch

Ingredients

2 mangoes

2 oz/55 g butter

1 oz/30 g golden sugar

$^1/_2$ cup porridge oats

7 oz/200 g carton full-fat farmer's cheese

7 oz/200 g carton heavy cream

juice of $^1/_2$ lemon

4 tbsp clear honey

Method

1 To prepare the mangoes, slice the 2 fatter 'cheeks' of the mangoes from either side of the stone. Cut a criss-cross pattern across the flesh of each piece to divide into small cubes, then push the skin upwards from the center and carefully slice off the cubes into a bowl.

2 Melt the butter and sugar in a saucepan and add the porridge oats. Cook over a medium heat for 4–5 minutes, stirring all the time, until the oats are just golden and toasted. Leave to cool slightly.

3 Mix together the farmer's cheese and heavy cream in a bowl, add the lemon juice, and 2 tablespoons of the honey, and combine well. Spoon the oats into individual glasses or serving bowls. Add a layer of the cream mixture, top with the mango, then drizzle over the remaining honey and serve straight away. Alternatively, fold the mango and oats into the cream and serve all combined in glasses or bowls.

Serves 4

Melon Filled with Melon Balls

Ingredients

1 cantaloupe melon

¹/₄ watermelon

¹/₂ honeydew melon

juice 1 lemon, lime, or orange

sugar to taste, optional

Method

1 Cut the cantaloupe carefully into 3 even sized wedges. Scoop out the seeds, and leaving the flesh in the shell and holding 1 at a time in a hand, press the open side of the melon baller firmly into the flesh until the rounded side touches it. Twist the baller to cut out a neat ball of flesh. Do this until all the flesh is gone, then use a spoon to scrape out the remaining pieces still clinging to the shell, to tidy it up for serving.

2 Flick out as many of the black seeds of the watermelon as possible, and leaving it in 1 piece, scoop out the flesh the same way. Prepare the honeydew melon the same way. Toss the melon balls in the fruit juice and sweeten to taste if desired.

3 Make a thin cut along 1 side of each of the cantaloupe shells, almost to the center. Then make another cut from the other end of the same side, almost to the center. Curl each of these cuts and hitch under the center piece to hold and form a bow. Fill these shells with the melon balls to serve.

Serves 6

Passionfruit Ice Cream with Cookie Hearts

Ingredients

7 fl oz/200 mL luxury vanilla ice cream

2 passion fruit

Cookie Hearts

**3¹/₂ oz/100 g butter, softened,
   plus extra for greasing**

¹/₄ cup confectioners' sugar, sifted

yolk of 1 small egg

5 oz/145 g all-purpose flour, sifted

¹/₄ cup ground almonds

Fruit Sauce

**¹/₄ cup fresh redcurrants
   or blackcurrants**

**2 tbsp redcurrant jelly or
   blackcurrant jelly**

1 tbsp confectioners' sugar

**3 tbsp crème de cassis (blackcurrant
   liqueur) or 1¹/₂ tbsp brandy mixed
   with 1 tbsp jelly**

Method

1 Take the ice cream out of the freezer and place in the refridgerator for 5–10 minutes to soften slightly. Halve 1 passionfruit and mix the pulp and seeds with the ice cream. Spoon into a freezer container and freeze for at least 1 hour.

2 Preheat the oven to 350°F/180°C/Gas Mark 4. To make the cookies, beat the butter and confectioners' sugar until pale and creamy. Beat in the egg yolk. Combine the flour and ground almonds, then stir into the mixture to form a ball of dough. Roll out on a lightly floured board to a thickness of ¹/₂ in/1 cm. Stamp out 10–12 cookies with a heart-shaped cutter, place on a greased baking sheet, and refrigerate for 15 minutes. Bake for 10 minutes or until golden.

3 Place the redcurrants or blackcurrants, jelly or jam, and 3 fl oz/75 mL of water in a small saucepan. Bring to a simmer, then press through a sieve into a bowl. Stir in the confectioners' sugar and crème de cassis or brandy mixture. Cool for 15 minutes. To serve, pour the sauce into bowls and top with ice cream. Halve the remaining passionfruit and spoon the pulp and seeds over the ice cream. Serve each portion with 2 cookies, storing the rest in an airtight tin.

Serves 2

Shrubbery

Ingredients

5 oz/145 g pack green jelly

1 tbsp lemon yogurt

7 oz/200 g soft fruit such as raspberries, blackberries, and strawberries

Method

1 Make the jelly as directed on the packet, but with 2 cups water. Cool for 2 hours, then refrigerate for 1–2 hours, until almost set. Whisk in the yogurt, then place in the refridgerator for 8 hours or until set.

2 Cut the jelly into cubes, dipping the knife into water to stop the jelly sticking. Pile the cubes into bowls, then scatter the fruit over the top.

Serves 4

Sticky Coconut Rice with Tropical Fruits

Ingredients

3 cups white rice

water

2$^1/_2$ cups coconut milk with $^1/_2$ cup of the cream skimmed from it and reserved

$^1/_2$ cup sugar

fresh bananas or mango, peeled and sliced

$^1/_2$ cup toasted shredded coconut

Method

1 Soak the rice overnight in just enough water to cover. Strain the rice in a metal colander and place it over a saucepan of simmering water. Cover tightly and steam the rice for 45 minutes, until the grains may be pressed between 2 fingers and no hard core is felt.

2 Now place the rice in a heavy sauce pan with the coconut milk and sugar. Cook over a gentle heat, stirring occasionally until all the coconut milk is absorbed. Turn on to a plate, flatten slightly, then allow to cool.

3 To serve, using 2 spoons, heap a mound of sticky rice on each plate and arrange the sliced fruit decoratively alongside it. Spoon a little of the reserved coconut cream over each mound and sprinkle with the toasted coconut.

Serves 6–8

Stir-Fried Fruit with Lychee and Lemongrass Ice Cream

Ingredients

¼ cup apple juice

I tbsp finely grated fresh ginger
or finely chopped ginger

I tbsp palm or brown sugar
or honey

2–3 cups seasonal fresh
fruit of your choice
(e.g. berries, paya, pineapple, kiwi fruit,
guava, mango, and banana)

½ cup white wine

¼ cup slivered unsalted
almonds, toasted

2 tbsp shredded fresh mint

I quantity lychee and lemongrass
ice cream or other ice cream
of your choice

Method

1 Place the apple juice, ginger, and sugar in a wok or nonstick frying pan over a medium heat. Cook, stirring, until the sugar melts and the sauce starts to thicken to a syrup.

2 Add the fruit. Stir-fry for 1–2 minutes. Stir in the wine. Cover and steam for 2–3 minutes. Scatter with the almonds and mint.

3 Serve immediately with the lychee and lemongrass ice cream.

Serves 6

Summer Pudding with Redcurrant Sauce

Ingredients

**2¼ lb/1 kg fresh or frozen
  mixed berry fruits**

3 tbsp superfine sugar

**8 slices white or whole-wheat bread,
  crusts removed**

2 tbsp redcurrant jelly

Method

1 Place the fruit, sugar and 3 tablespoons, of water in a saucepan and simmer for 5 minutes or until the fruit has softened. Leave to cool slightly.

2 Line the base and sides of a 4-cup capacity pudding basin with 6 slices of the bread, cutting to fit and making sure there are no gaps. Strain the fruit, reserving the juice, then add the fruit to the basin. Cover with the remaining bread to form a lid. Spoon over 3–4 tablespoons of the reserved juice.

3 Place a plate on top of the bread, with a weight, such as a large can, on it. Place in the refridgerator for 2–3 hours to let the juices soak through the bread.

4 For the sauce, strain the reserved juice into a sauce pan, then add the redcurrant jelly. Simmer for 2–3 minutes, stirring, until the jelly has melted. Invert the pudding onto a plate and serve with the redcurrant sauce.

Serves 6

In this section, you will find comforting, warming desserts to finish a meal well. Winter is a time for strong flavors and hearty, satisfying food. Use these recipes to complete a meal with a trully perfect dessert for the season.

Winter Favorites

Winter
Favorites

Banana Filo Tart

Ingredients

**6 large sheets filo pastry, defrosted,
if frozen, trimmed to 10 x
12 in/25 cm x 13 in/30 cm**

2 oz/55 g sweet butter, melted

3 large bananas, sliced

4 dried figs, sliced

I heaped tbsp superfine sugar

pinch of ground apple spice

grated rind of ½ lemon

I tbsp dark rum

Method

1 Preheat the oven to 400°F/200°C/Gas Mark 6. Place a baking sheet on the top shelf to heat.

2 Brush a sheet of filo pastry with the butter. Top with a second sheet and brush it with the butter. Repeat with the remaining sheets until all the pastry has been used, then transfer to a cold baking sheet.

3 Arrange the banana and fig slices over the pastry sheets, then scatter over the sugar, apple spice, and lemon rind. Pour over the rum and any remaining butter. Carefully transfer the tart to the heated baking sheet using a fish slice, and bake for 15 minutes, or until golden and bubbling.

Serves 4

Apricot and Lime Soufflé

Ingredients

9 oz/255 g pack ready-to-eat
  dried apricots
1 mint tea bag
finely grated rind and juice
  of 2 limes
butter for greasing
6 tbsp golden superfine sugar,
  plus extra for coating
6 large egg whites
pinch of salt
confectioners' sugar for dusting

Method

1 Place the apricots and the tea bag in a bowl, cover with boiling water, and leave to soak for 1 hour. Drain, reserving 2$\frac{1}{2}$ tablespoons of the liquid, and discard the tea bag. Put the apricots in a food processor with the reserved liquid, lime rind, and juice and blend to a slightly chunky purée. Transfer to a large bowl.

2 Butter a 8 in/20 cm soufflé dish and dust with the superfine sugar. Heat the oven to 375°F/190°C/Gas Mark 5. Whisk the egg whites with a tiny pinch of salt until they form soft peaks (this is easiest with an electric whisk). Gradually sprinkle in the sugar and whisk again until the mixture is thick and glossy.

3 Using a large metal spoon, fold a spoonful of the whisked egg whites into the apricot purée to loosen it, then gently fold in the rest of the egg whites. Spoon the mixture into the soufflé dish. Cook for 30–35 minutes, until just firm and well risen. Dust the soufflé with the confectioners' sugar and serve immediately.

Serves 4

Apple Cake with Maple Sauce

Ingredients

1 Granny Smith apple or
  ¹/₂ cup apple purée
3 large Granny Smith apples, extra
3 cups all-purpose flour
3 tsp baking powder
1 tsp apple spice
¹/₂ tsp nutmeg
2 cups sugar
¹/₂ tsp salt
4 oz/115 g firm butter
3 large eggs
¹/₂ cup peanut oil
2 tsp vanilla extract

Sauce
  1 cup Canadian maple syrup
  ¹/₂ cup thick cream
  2 oz/55 g butter
  good pinch of salt
  ice cream

Method

1 Preheat the oven to 350°F/180°C/Gas Mark 4 and generously grease a babka tin or 8 in/20 cm round tin with a central funnel. Dust with flour and set aside.

2 If you are using a fresh apple to make the purée, peel, core, and chop the apple and simmer with 2 tablespoons of water until very soft. Purée or fork mash the apple. Peel, core, and dice the remaining 3 apples.

3 In a bowl, mix together the flour, apple spice, nutmeg, sugar, and salt. Rub the butter through with your fingertips until the mixture resembles fine breadcrumbs.

4 In a separate bowl, whisk together the eggs, oil, and vanilla until smooth. Add the puréed apple and mix well. Using a wooden spoon, combine the flour mixture with the egg mixture, then fold in the diced apple pieces. Pour the batter into the prepared tin, then bake for 45–50 minutes or until golden and firm on top. Remove the cake from the oven and allow to cool in the tin, then gently turn out.

5 To make the syrup, mix together the syrup, cream, butter, and salt, and bring to the boil. Simmer for 2 minutes, then cool slightly. Serve the syrup spooned around the cake, with a scoop of vanilla ice cream or pure cream.

Serves 8–10

Black Rice Pudding

Ingredients

1½ cups black glutinous rice

4–4½ cups water

1 pandan leaf

½ cup Palm Sugar Syrup

coconut milk or ice cream to serve

Palm Sugar Syrup

1 cup grated palm sugar
  or brown sugar

½ cup water

Method

1 Rinse the rice under cold running water for 1–2 minutes or until the water runs clear.

2 Combine the rice, water, and pandan leaf in a large saucepan. Bring to the boil and simmer over a low heat for 40 minutes. Add the syrup and cook for a further 10 minutes or until the rice is tender and the liquid has been absorbed.

3 To make the palm sugar syrup, combine the sugar and water in a small saucepan. Bring to the boil and simmer for 8–10 minutes.

4 Serve the pudding with the coconut milk or ice cream.

Serves 4–6

Caramel Praline Soufflé

Ingredients

**butter and sugar for preparing
   soufflé dishes**

1 cup milk

1½ oz/45 g sugar

1½ oz/45 g all-purpose flour

1 tbsp butter

3 egg yolks

½ cup Vienna almonds, ground

2 tsp rum

4 egg whites

1½ tbsp sugar

**⅓ cup Vienna almonds,
   roughly chopped**

confectioners' sugar to serve

Method

1   Prepare the soufflé dishes by lightly brushing them with the melted butter, and then sprinkling the sugar around the sides and base of the dish. Tip out any excess.

2   Remove 3 tablespoons of milk (from the 1 cup) and heat the remaining milk. In a mixing bowl, place the 1½ oz/45 g of sugar, the flour, and the reserved 3 tablespoons of milk, and whisk together. Add a little of the heated milk, whisking continuously, then pour the entire mixture into the saucepan containing the remaining milk. Heat gently and simmer for 2 minutes. Add the butter, then cover the saucepan and allow to cool for 15 minutes. Stir in the egg yolks (mixing well), then add the ground almonds and rum.

3   Preheat the oven to 400°F/200°C/Gas Mark 6.

4   In a separate bowl, whisk the egg whites until they are very soft. Add the 1½ tablespoons of sugar and continue beating until the egg whites are firm, but not dry. Fold gently into the batter.

5   Pour the batter into the prepared dishes until they are ⅓ full, then sprinkle the roughly chopped Vienna almonds over the surface. Pour the remaining batter over the almonds and fill the soufflé dishes ¾ full.

6   Bake for 12–15 minutes or until set but slightly "wobbly". Dust with confectioners' sugar and serve.

Serves 6–8

Caramelized Milk

Ingredients

I cup sugar

8 egg yolks

¹/₃ cup cornstarch

5 cups milk

¹/₂ cup almond meal

I tbsp vanilla extract

pinch ground cinnamon

fruit of your choice to serve

Sugar Topping

¹/₂ cup sugar

I oz/30 g butter

Method

1   Place the sugar and egg yolks in a bowl and beat until thick and creamy. Blend the cornstarch with ¹/₂ cup of the milk. Beat almond meal, remaining milk, cornstarch mixture, vanilla extract, and cinnamon into the egg mixture. Pour the mixture into a saucepan and cook over a low heat, stirring constantly, until the mixture boils and thickens.

2 Pour the mixture into a heatproof serving dish, cover the surface with a piece of greased baking paper, and chill for several hours or until set.

3 To make the sugar topping, remove the paper from the top of the pudding, then sprinkle with the sugar and dot with the butter. Heat a comal or large metal spoon over a high heat for 10 minutes or until very hot. Run the comal or spoon over the topping until the sugar caramelizes. Serve immediately decorated with fresh fruit of your choice.

Serves 8

Champagne and Strawberry Risotto

Ingredients

2 1/3 cups water

5 oz/145g sugar

2 tbsp butter

7 oz/200 g strawberries, chopped

14 oz/400g arborio rice

2 cups champagne

7 oz/200g strawberries

1 1/2 tbsp strawberry syrup or liquor

savionie cookies to serve

Method

1 Mix the water and sugar together in a small saucepan and bring to the boil. Simmer gently while you begin the risotto.

2 Heat the butter and sauté the chopped strawberries until softened.

3 Add the rice and stir to coat, cooking for 1–2 minutes or two until the butter has been absorbed by the rice. Add the champagne and simmer until there is no alcoholic aroma wafting from the pan, and the rice has absorbed the liquid.

4 Begin to add the sugar syrup, 1 cup at a time, stirring well after each addition and allowing the liquid to be absorbed before the next addition.

5 When all the sugar syrup has been absorbed, remove the sauce pan from the heat. Add the remaining strawberries and strawberry syrup and stir well. Serve immediately over savionie cookies, with a little extra syrup spooned over the top.

Serves 4

Citrus Risotto

Ingredients

2 tbsp butter

4 tbsp sugar

zest of 1 lime

zest of 1 lemon

zest of 1 orange

14 oz/400 g arborio rice

¹/₃ cup white wine

3¹/₄ cups orange juice, simmering

2 oranges, segmented and chopped

juice of 1 lemon

juice of 1 lime

2 tbsp raw sugar*

¹/₄ cup toasted flaked almonds

***available from Asian food stores**

Method

1 In a saucepan, add the butter, sugar, and all the zests. Stir well and sauté until the mixture is bubbling and fragrant.

2 Add the rice, stir well, and cook for 2 minutes.

3 Add the white wine and mix well, allowing all the alcohol to evaporate and the liquid to be absorbed by the rice. Add 1 cup of orange juice and stir while the rice simmers in the juice. When the rice begins to look a little dry, add the next cup of juice and stir well again. Continue in this fashion until all the juice has been added and absorbed and the rice is tender.

4 Stir through the orange segments, juice of lemon and lime, and raw sugar, and garnish with the toasted almonds.

Serves 4

English Baked Rice Pudding

Ingredients

5 cups milk

2 tbsp light cream

butter for greasing

1 cup short-grain rice

1 oz/30 g sugar

grated peel of ¹/₂ lemon

¹/₂ tsp grated nutmeg

Method

1 Preheat oven to 300°F/150°C/Gas Mark 2

2 Heat the milk and cream but do not boil. Butter a 4 cup pie dish. Mix the rice with the milk and pour into the pie dish. Leave it to stand for 20 minutes.

3 Stir in the sugar and lemon peel and sprinkle the top with the nutmeg. Bake in the oven for 2 hours. Stir well every half an hour.

Serves 4

Fig and Rhubarb Risotto

Ingredients

1½ cups orange juice

2½ cups water

5½ oz/155 g sugar

8 ribs rhubarb, red part only

2 tbsp butter

10 dried figs, halved

14 oz/400 g arborio rice

1 tbsp marscarpone cheese

4–6 fresh figs

1 tbsp brown sugar

Method

1 Mix the orange juice, water, and sugar together, and simmer for 10 minutes.

2 Wash and slice the rhubarb into ³/₄ in/2 cm pieces. Heat the butter, and add the rhubarb and figs, and sauté for 3 minutes.

3 Add the rice and stir to coat. When the rice is shiny, begin adding the syrup/juice mixture, 1 cup at a time. Stir well to incorporate the ingredients. When the liquid has been absorbed and the rice is a little dry, add the next addition of syrup and stir well.

4 Continue in this fashion until all the liquid has been absorbed and the rice is tender.

5 Add the marscarpone cheese and stir well.

6 Cut the fresh figs in half and sprinkle a little brown sugar on each cut surface. Broil the fruit, sugar-side up, until caramelized, about 2 minutes, then serve on top of the risotto in individual bowls.

Serves 4

Flourless Poppyseed Cake

Ingredients

4 large eggs, separated

4¹/₂ oz/125 g butter, softened

grated zest of 1 lemon

¹/₂ cup confectioners' sugar

2 tbsp Dutch cocoa

¹/₄ cup superfine sugar

6 oz/170 g poppy seeds

extra confectioners' sugar to serve

Method

1 Preheat the oven to 335°F/170°C/Gas Mark 3 and butter a 9¹/₂ in/24 cm round cake tin. Set aside.

2 In the bowl of an electric mixer, beat the egg yolks, soft butter, grated lemon zest, and confectioners' sugar until thick and smooth, about 5 minutes. Fold in the cocoa and mix well.

3 Meanwhile, beat the egg whites until 'foamy', raise the speed, and sprinkle in the superfine sugar while the eggs are beating. Continue until the egg whites are thick and glossy.

4 Mix the poppyseeds into the yolk mixture, then add the egg whites, and combine gently.

5 Spoon the batter into the prepared tin and smooth the top.

6 Bake at for 70 minutes. Remove the cake from the oven and allow to cool in the tin.

7 When the cake is cold, remove from the tin and dust with the confectioners' sugar. For a more decorative finish, cut strips of paper and lay these over the cake before dusting with the confectioners' sugar.

Serves 10–12

Fruit Gratin

Ingredients

8 egg yolks

9 oz/255 g sugar

3 cups light cream

1 tsp kirsch liqueur

cream

2¼ lb/1 kg mixed fresh fruit, cut into
pieces and any stones

Method

1 Beat the egg yolks with the sugar. Heat the cream in a saucepan to boiling point, then stir into the egg and sugar mixture. Return it all to the saucepan and stir until the mixture boils. Flavor with the kirsch.

2 Pour the cream over the fruit and broil for a few seconds. Serve immediately.

Serves 8

Grand Marnier Soufflé

Ingredients

¹/₂ cup orange juice

1 tsp grated orange rind

³/₄ cup cooked long-grain rice

4 egg yolks

1 tbsp superfine sugar

1 tbsp cornstarch

1¹/₄ cups milk

4 tbsp Grand Marnier

5 egg whites

¹/₃ cup superfine sugar, extra

Method

1 Place the orange juice, rind and rice in a saucepan and bring to the boil. Reduce the heat and allow to simmer, stirring occasionally, until all of liquid has been absorbed. Set aside

2 Whisk together the egg yolks, superfine sugar, and cornstarch. Heat the milk in a saucepan until just at boiling point. Add to the egg yolk the mixture, whisk, then return mixture to the saucepan. Stir over a medium heat until the custard boils and thickens. Reduce the heat and simmer for 3–4 minutes, stirring constantly. Remove from the heat. Stir in the Grand Marnier and the rice mixture. Cool slightly.

3 Preheat the oven to 440°F/220°C/Gas Mark 7. Beat the egg whites until stiff peaks form. Add the extra sugar, a tablespoon at a time, beating after each addition. Stir a little beaten egg white into the rice custard, then lightly fold in the remaining whites. Spoon into the prepared soufflé dish. Bake for 20–25 minutes until the soufflé is puffed and golden. Serve immediately.

Serves 4

Macaroon-Stuffed Peaches

Ingredients

8 large firm 'freestone' peaches

3¹/₂ oz/100 g butter

7 oz/200 g superfine sugar

3¹/₂ fl oz/100 mL red wine

9 oz/255 g coconut macaroons

¹/₂ cup coarse matzoh meal
   or dry breadcrumbs

1 cup milk

2 tbsp sugar, extra

1 egg

2 raw sugar

cream or vanilla ice cream to serve

Method

1 Preheat the oven to 500°F/250°C/Gas Mark 4.

2 Cut the peaches in ¹/₂ and remove the stones. Melt the butter, add the sugar and the wine, and stir gently until the sugar dissolves. Add the peach halves, cut-side down in the syrup, and cook on a low heat for about 10 minutes. Turn the peaches once towards the end of the cooking time.

3 Remove the peaches from the syrup, and then boil the syrup to reduce. Take care not to allow the syrup to burn. Spoon 1 dessertspoon of the syrup over each peach.

4 Crush the macaroons and set aside. Soak the matzoh meal with the milk and 2 tablespoons of the sugar. When the matzoh has absorbed the milk, add the crushed macaroons and the egg. Mix well.

5 Spoon this filling into the peach cavities and sprinkle with the raw sugar. Bake at for 10 minutes, then broil briefly, if desired to melt sugar. Serve with the cream or vanilla ice cream.

Serves 8

Mango Cake with Nutmeg Cream

Ingredients

I cup unsalted, roasted
   macadamia nuts

3 large mangoes, about I^2/$_3$ lb/750 g

9 oz/255 g butter, softened

I tsp vanilla extract

I cup superfine sugar

4 large eggs

2 cups all-purpose flour

I^1/$_2$ tsp baking powder

^{1}/$_2$ cup roasted macadamia
   nuts, chopped

confectioners' sugar

2 cups pure cream

I tsp nutmeg

I mango, sliced, for serving

Method

1 Preheat the oven to 350°F/180°C/Gas Mark 4, and grease a 9 in/22 cm non stick cake tin with butter.

2 Crush the roasted macadamia nuts in a food processor and set aside.

3 Peel the mangoes and dice the flesh, saving as much juice as possible, then reserve some pieces of mango (about 3 oz/85 g) and purée the remaining mango flesh with all the reserved juice. You should have about I cup of mango purée.

4 Beat the softened butter and vanilla extract with ^{1}/$_2$ the sugar. Beat until thick and pale. While beating, add the remaining sugar and beat until all the sugar has been added. Add the eggs, I at a time, and beat well after each addition.

5 In a separate bowl, combine the crushed nuts, flour, and baking powder.

6 Remove the bowl from the mixer and add the flour mixture, stirring well to combine. Add the mango purée and mix gently.

7 Spoon the batter into the prepared tin, then sprinkle the chopped macadamia nuts and reserved diced mango over the batter and swirl through.

8 Bake for I hour, then remove the cake from the oven and cool in the tin. When cool, remove from the tin and dredge with the confectioners' sugar.

9 To prepare the cream, whip the cream and nutmeg together until the cream is thick and fragrant. Serve alongside the cake with some mango slices.

Serves 6

Rice Pudding

Ingredients

20 cups milk

4¹/₂ oz/125 g butter

1 lb/455 g Spanish short-grain rice

1 tsp salt

2 cinnamon sticks

1 lb/455 g sugar

powdered cinnamon

Method

1 Bring the milk to the boil in 2 or more saucepans. Let it cool.

2 Put the butter in a very large saucepan (not aluminium) over a gentle heat. When it starts to soften, brush the butter up the sides, then add the boiled cooked milk, rice, salt, and cinnamon sticks. Bring to the boil, and then lower the heat, and cook gently, stirring frequently with a wooden spoon until it is done, about 2 hours.

3 Just before the rice is ready, stir in the sugar. Leave the pudding to rest for about 10 minutes before serving sprinkled with the powdered cinnamon. Well worth the time and trouble!

Serves 6

Risotto of Nectarine, Basil, and Pine Nuts

Ingredients

2 tbsp butter

4 firm nectarines, sliced

4 fresh basil leaves, finely shredded

1 tsp balsamic vinegar

1¹/₂ cup apricot nectar

1¹/₂ cups water

¹/₃ cup orange juice

14 oz/400 g arborio rice

¹/₃ cup white wine

2 tbsp brown sugar

3 tbsp pine nuts

3 tbsp light sour cream

3 basil leaves, finely shredded

Method

1 In a saucepan, heat the butter and add the nectarine slices and basil leaves. Sauté until the fruit is golden, then add the balsamic vinegar. Stir well, then remove the nectarines and set aside.

2 Combine the apricot nectar, water, and orange juice and heat to simmering.

3 To the remaining hot butter, add the arborio rice and stir well to coat. Add the white wine and simmer until the liquid has been absorbed and the alcohol has evaporated.

4 Add 1 cup of the juice mixture and the brown sugar, and stir well, allowing the rice to simmer until all the liquid has been absorbed, before adding the next quantity of juice.

5 When all the juice has been added and absorbed, remove the risotto from the heat and serve in individual bowls, with the nectarine mixture over the top and garnished with the toasted pine nuts, sour cream, and finely shredded basil leaves.

Serves 4

Rice Tyrolhof with Apricot Sauce

Ingredients

Rice

7 oz/200 g short-grain rice

1½ cups milk

2 eggs, separated

2 tbsp superfine sugar

1 orange

**1 tbsp finely chopped candied
   peel, optional**

2 tsp gelatine

1 dessert apple, diced

**3 oz/85 g strawberries or grapes, sliced
   extra whole strawberries to serve**

**1 tbsp finely chopped candied
   peel, optional**

Apricot Sauce

5 oz/145 g apricot jelly

1 tbsp lemon juice

2 tsp lemon rind

3 tbsp hot water

Method

1 Combine all the sauce ingredients and chill.

2 Simmer the rice the with milk until soft and creamy, 25–30 minutes. Remove from heat. Beat the egg yolks with the sugar and stir into the rice. Add 2 teaspoons of the grated orange rind and candied peel.

3 Dissolve the gelatine in the orange juice over hot water and add to the rice with the fruit. When cool, add beaten the egg whites and pour into a serving dish. Chill. Serve with the apricot sauce, topped with extra whole strawberries.

Serves 6

Bakewell Tart with Plums

Ingredients

6 oz/170 g all-purpose flour

1¹/₃ oz/40 g confectioners' sugar

3 oz/85 g butter, diced

1 medium egg yolk

juice of ¹/₂ lemon

Filling

**1 lb/455 g plums, halved,
   stoned and chopped**

6 oz/170 g superfine sugar

4 oz/115 g sweet butter, softened

2 medium eggs, beaten

5 oz/145 g ground almonds

**few drops almond extract,
   optional**

2 oz/55 g flaked almonds

Method

1 Sift the flour and confectioners' sugar into a bowl, add the butter and rub in using your fingertips until the mixture resembles fine breadcrumbs. Add the egg yolk and lemon juice and mix to a dough. Cover and refrigerate for 30 minutes.

2 Preheat the oven to 375°F/190°C/Gas Mark 5. Use the pastry to line a deep 8 in/20 cm metal flan tin. Line with baking paper and baking beans, then bake blind for 10–12 minutes, until the pastry is golden. Set aside, then reduce the oven temperature to 350°F/180°C/Gas Mark 4.

3 Cook the plums with 2 oz/55 g of sugar in a saucepan for 10 minutes or until soft. Cool, drain, discarding the syrup, then spread over the pastry case. Beat the butter and remaining sugar together, until light and fluffy. Beat in the eggs a little at a time, then beat in the ground almonds and extract if using. Smooth the filling over the plums, sprinkle with the flaked almonds, then bake for 50 minutes or until the filling is set.

Serves 4

Apple Pie

Ingredients

- **1 tbsp softened butter, plus extra for greasing**
- **1 tbsp all-purpose flour, plus extra for sprinkling**
- **1 lb/455 g ready-made shortcrust pastry, defrosted if frozen**
- **2 oz/55 g granulated sugar**
- **1/2 tsp ground cinnamon**
- **1/2 tsp apple spice**
- **2 1/4 lb/1 kg cooking apples, peeled, cored and cut into thick slices**
- **1 tbsp milk**
- **1 tbsp superfine sugar**

Method

1 Preheat the oven to 375°F/190°C/Gas Mark 5. Grease a 10 in/25 cm pie dish with the butter, using a folded kitchen towel. Divide the pastry in 1/2 and put 1 1/2 in the refrigerator to keep cool while you work with the other 1/2.

2 Sprinkle the work surface and a rolling pin with the flour. Roll the pastry into a rough circle 1 1/2 in/4 cm larger in diameter than the pie dish. Lift the pastry and drape it over the rolling pin to help you ease it into the pie dish. Trim off any excess pastry. Place the dish in the refrigerator for 15 minutes.

3 Mix together the sugar, cinnamon, apple spice, and the 1 tablespoon of flour. Arrange the apples on top of the pastry, sprinkle with the spice mixture, and dot with the butter.

4 Roll out the second 1/2 of pastry in the same way as the first. Moisten the edges of the pastry in the pie dish with water. Drape the pastry top over the apples and press the edges of the pastry base and top together to seal. Trim off any excess pastry and discard, then pinch the pastry edge between your thumb and first finger to crimp it. Make 2 deep cuts in the center of the pie to create steam vents.

5 Brush the top of the pie lightly with the milk and sprinkle with the superfine sugar. Bake for 45–60 minutes, until the pastry is golden and the apples are tender when pierced with a knife.

Serves 6

Blackcurrant and Lemon Soufflés

Ingredients

6 oz/170 g blackcurrants

3½ oz/100 g superfine sugar

1 tbsp cassis or other fruit liqueur

2 oz/55 g butter, softened,
  plus extra for greasing

finely grated zest and juice
  of 1 lemon

3 medium eggs, separated

3½ oz/100 g cream cheese

confectioner' sugar to dust

Method

1 Preheat the oven to 375°F/190°C/Gas Mark 5. Place the blackcurrants in a small saucepan with 2 oz/55 g of the sugar and cook for 3 minutes or until they begin to split. Stir in the cassis or other fruit liqueur, then set aside. Lightly grease 4 x ½ cup-capacity ramekins with butter.

2 Beat the butter with the remaining sugar until pale and creamy. Beat in the lemon rind and juice, egg yolks, and cream cheese. Whisk the egg whites until they form stiff peaks (this is best done with an electric whisk). Carefully fold a spoonful of the egg whites into the cream cheese mixture to loosen, then fold in the rest.

3 Divide the blackcurrant mixture between the ramekins and top with the cream cheese mixture. Bake for 30 minutes or until risen and firm. Dust the soufflés with the confectioners' sugar and serve immediately.

Serves 4

Extra-Light Banana Clafoutis

Ingredients

3 oz/85 g butter, melted

**3 tbsp molasses or soft dark
  brown sugar**

grated rind and juice of 1 lemon

3 tbsp rum

2 lb/900 g bananas, cut into chunks

1 cup half-fat milk

4 eggs, separated

3 tbsp sugar

1/2 cup all-purpose flour

1 tsp ground cinnamon

confectioners' sugar to dust

Method

1 Preheat the oven to 450°F/230°C/Gas Mark 8. Place the melted butter, molasses or sugar, lemon rind and juice, and the rum in a 13 x 9 in/33 x 23 cm ovenproof dish and mix well. Add the bananas and toss to coat. Cook for 12–15 minutes, basting frequently, until the bananas have softened.

2 Meanwhile, gently warm the milk in a small saucepan. Beat the egg yolks and sugar until pale and creamy. Beat in the warmed milk, then the flour and cinnamon. Whisk the whites until they form soft peaks, then fold gently into the mixture.

3 Remove the bananas from the oven and reduce the temperature to 400°F/200°C/Gas Mark 6. Pour the batter over the bananas and return the dish to the oven. Bake for 20–25 minutes, until browned and well risen. Check the pudding is cooked by inserting a skewer into the center; it should come out clean. Allow to cool slightly – the mixture will sink rapidly as it cools – then dust with the confectioners' sugar and serve warm.

Serves 6

French Bread Pudding

Ingredients

I loaf brioche, sliced

6 eggs, lightly beaten

1 1/2 cups milk

I tsp vanilla extract

I tsp ground nutmeg

Fruit Filling

4 oz/115 g dried figs, chopped

4 oz/115 g dried dates,
  pitted and chopped

1/2 cup orange juice

1/3 cup brandy

I cinnamon stick

Method

1 To make the filling, place the figs, dates, orange juice, brandy, and cinnamon stick in a saucepan and cook over a low heat, stirring, for 15–20 minutes or until the fruit is soft and mixture thick. Remove the cinnamon stick.

2 To assemble pudding, place 1/3 of the brioche slices in the base of a greased 11x 4 1/2 in/21 cm x 8 1/2 in loaf tin. Top with half the filling. Repeat layers, ending with a layer of the brioche.

3 Place the eggs, milk, vanilla extract and nutmeg in a bowl and whisk to combine. Carefully pour the egg mixture over the brioche and fruit and set aside to stand for 5 minutes. Place the tin in a baking dish with enough boiling water to come halfway up the sides of the tin and bake for 45 minutes or until firm. Stand the pudding in the tin for 10 minutes before turning out and serving.

Note: This tempting dessert is best eaten cut into slices and served with cream shortly after it is turned out of the tin.

Serves 6–8

Hedgerow Pie

Ingredients

**9 oz/255 g fresh or frozen mixed
fruits, such as blackberries,
raspberries, blueberries, and
strawberries**

**1 oz/30 g superfine sugar, plus
extra for dusting**

5 oz/145 g shortcrust pastry

1 egg, beaten, for glazing

Method

1 Preheat the oven to 200°C/400°F/Gas Mark 6. Put the fruit and sugar into a saucepan. Simmer, covered, for 1–2 minutes, until the fruit begins to soften, then leave for 5 minutes to cool. Strain the fruit, reserving the juice.

2 Set aside a small piece of pastry to make the decorations. Roll out the remaining pastry on a floured surface into a rough circle, about 7 in/18 cm across. Place on a non stick baking sheet. Put the fruit in the center of the pastry and gather up the edges, leaving the top slightly open. Brush the top of the pastry with a little of the egg.

3 Roll out the reserved pastry and cut out acorn, leaf and blackberry shapes. Brush the shapes with the egg and stick them onto the sides of the pie. Bake for 25 minutes or until the pastry is golden. Remove from the oven. Lightly dust with the superfine sugar. Serve with the reserved fruit juice, if desired.

Serves 2

Homemade Apple Pie

Ingredients

egg white or water to glaze

extra sugar

Pastry

2¹/₂ cups all-purpose flour

pinch salt

¹/₂ tsp baking powder

6¹/₂ oz/185 g sweet butter

1 tbsp sugar

1 egg yolk

1 tbsp cold water

Filling

6–7 cooking apples

¹/₂ cup sugar

2 tbsp all-purpose flour

1 tsp ground cinnamon

Method

1 Sift the flour with the salt and baking powder into a bowl. Cut the butter into small pieces and rub into the flour until mixture resembles breadcrumbs. Stir in the sugar. Make a well in the center and add the egg yolk and water. Blend into the dry ingredients to make a firm dough. Knead very lightly and form into a ball. Wrap and chill in the refrigerator for about 30 minutes.

2 Meanwhile, peel and core the apples and slice thinly. Combine the sugar, flour, and cinnamon and mix with the apple slices. Cut a ¹/₃ off the pastry and reserve for the top of the pie. Roll out the remaining pastry on a lightly floured surface and line a 9 in/23 cm pie dish. Spoon the apples into the pastry case. Roll the remaining pastry to cover the pie. Press the edges together, trim, and press the edge in flutes. Brush with the slightly beaten egg white or water and with a pointed knife make steam vents on top of the pie. Dust the pie lightly with the extra sugar.

3 Bake in a preheated moderately hot oven for 1–1¹/₂ hours. Reduce the heat if the pastry begins to darken. Serve hot or warm with whipped cream or ice cream.

Serves 6–8

Lemon and Golden Raisin Bread Pudding

Ingredients

1½ oz/45 g sunflower spread, plus
  extra for greasing

6 medium slices whole-wheat bread

1 cup golden raisins

finely grated zest of 1 small lemon

1½ oz/45 g soft light brown sugar

2 medium eggs

2¼ cups half-fat milk

Method

1 Lightly grease a 9 x 11 in/23 x 28 cm ovenproof dish. Spread 1 side of each bread slice with sunflower spread, then cut each slice into 4 triangles and arrange ½ of them in the base of the prepared dish, spread-side up.

2 Mix together the golden raisins, lemon zest, and ½ the sugar, then sprinkle over the bread. Arrange the remaining bread over the top, spread-side up, and sprinkle with the rest of the sugar.

3 Beat together the eggs and milk and pour over the bread. Set aside for 30 minutes to allow the bread to absorb some of the liquid. Meanwhile, preheat the oven to 350°F/180°C/Gas Mark 4. Bake in the oven for 45 minutes, until lightly set and golden brown.

Serves 4

Lemon Meringue Rice Pudding

Ingredients

3 oz/85 g pudding rice

2¼ cups whole milk

3½ oz/100 g superfine sugar

**2 strips of lemon zest, pared
  with a vegetable peeler**

⅔ cup carton whipping cream

3½ oz/100 g lemon curd

1 packet easy dried egg white

Method

1 Put the rice, milk, ½ oz/15 g of the sugar, and the lemon rind into a saucepan. Bring to the boil, then reduce the heat and simmer, uncovered, for 30 minutes until thick and creamy, stirring from time to time. Remove the lemon rind and set the rice aside for 1 hour or until completely cooled, stirring occasionally.

2 Preheat the oven to 400°F/200°C/Gas Mark 6. Whisk the cream until it forms soft peaks, then fold into the rice. Spread the lemon curd over the base of a 9 x 6 in/23 x 15 cm ovenproof dish. Spread the rice on top. Whisk the egg powder and 2 fl oz/55 mL of water together until foamy (this is easiest with an electric whisk). Gradually whisk in the remaining sugar until thick and glossy. Spoon over the rice.

3 Cook at the top of the oven for 10 minutes or until the meringue is crisp and golden brown. Leave to cool for 10 minutes before serving.

Serves 4

Liquid Lime

Ingredients

1 oz/30 g butter, plus extra
   for greasing
3^1/$_3$ oz/100 g superfine sugar
finely grated zest and juice
   of 2 limes
5 fl oz/145 mL whole milk
2 medium eggs, separated
1 oz/30 g all-purpose flour

Method

1 Preheat the oven to 375°F/190°C/Gas Mark 5. Beat the butter and sugar together. Add the lime rind and juice and beat well. Mix the milk and egg yolks in a separate bowl, then add to the creamed mixture with the flour and beat well.

2 Whisk the egg whites until they form stiff peaks (this is easiest with an electric whisk). Fold a spoonful into the creamed mixture to loosen it, then fold in the rest. Pour into a buttered 4 cup soufflé dish.

3 Place the dish on a double layer of newspaper in a deep roasting tin. Pour boiling water into the tin to reach halfway up the sides. Cook for 45 minutes, until well risen and firm.

Serves 4

Peach and Hazelnut Crumble

Ingredients

3 x 14¹/₂ fl oz/410 g cans
   peach halves in natural juice,
   drained but reserving
   7 fl oz/200 mL of juice
3 pieces preserved ginger
   in syrup, drained and
   finely chopped
3¹/₂ oz/100 g all-purpose flour
3¹/₂ oz/100 g roasted chopped
   hazelnuts
4 tbsp soft light brown sugar
1 tsp ground cinnamon
3¹/₂ oz/100 g butter, cubed

Method

1 Preheat the oven to 400°F/200°C/Gas Mark 6. Arrange the peaches, cut-side up, in a 12 x 10 in/30 x 25 cm ovenproof dish. Sprinkle with the ginger. Boil the reserved juice in a saucepan for 5 minutes or until reduced by ¹/₃. Pour over the peaches.

2 In a large bowl, mix together the flour, hazelnuts, sugar and cinnamon. Add the butter and rub in with the tips of your fingers until the mixture resembles fine breadcrumbs. Sprinkle over the fruit and bake for 30–35 minutes, until browned.

Serves 6

Peach Tea Cake

Ingredients

4¹/₂ oz/125 g butter

¹/₂ cup superfine sugar

2 eggs

1 tsp vanilla extract

2 cups all-purpose flour

2 tsp baking powder

¹/₂ cup sugar

¹/₂ tsp salt

¹/₂ cup milk

3 peeled peaches, sliced into thin wedges

cream or ice cream to serve

Topping

1 oz/30 g butter, melted

1 tsp ground cinnamon

2 tbsp sugar

Method

1 Butter a 9 in/23 cm round cake tin and line the base with greaseproof paper. Cream the butter until soft and gradually beat in the sugar until light and fluffy. Beat in the eggs, 1 at a time, incorporating the first thoroughly before adding the other. Beat in the vanilla extract. Sift the flour with the baking powder, sugar, and salt, and fold into the creamed mixture lightly and thoroughly with the milk. Fold with a large metal spoon.

2 Spread the mixture in the prepared tin evenly right to the edges. Now prepare the peaches and arrange in a circular pattern to cover the top of the cake, pressing thin edges into the dough. Brush with the melted butter, sprinkle with the cinnamon and sugar and bake in a moderately hot oven at 375°F/190°C/Gas Mark 5 for 40 minutes. Serve the cake warm, cut into wedges with cream or ice cream.

Serves 8

Pear, Raspberry, and Almond Sponge

Ingredients

7 fl oz/200 mL dry or slightly sweet white wine, such as Alsace Gewürztraminer

2–3 strips lemon zest, pared with a vegetable peeler, and juice of 1 lemon

2 tbsp clear honey or sugar

4 whole cloves

4 large ripe pears, peeled, quartered, and cored

3¹/₂ oz/100 g butter, softened

¹/₄ cup superfine sugar

grated rind of ¹/₂ orange

3 eggs, lightly beaten

5 oz/145 g ground almonds

2 tsp orange-flower water or natural vanilla extract, optional

4 oz/115 g carton fresh raspberries

sifted confectioners' sugar to dust

Method

1 Preheat the oven to 350°F/180°C/Gas Mark 4. Place the wine, lemon rind and juice, honey or sugar, and cloves in a saucepan. Bring to the boil, then simmer, uncovered, for 5 minutes or until reduced slightly. Add the pears, cover, and cook for 5 minutes or until tender. Transfer the pears to a dish, drain, and cool. Strain the cooking liquid, discarding the lemon rind and cloves, and reserve.

2 Beat the butter, sugar, and orange rind until light and fluffy (this is easiest with an electric whisk). Gradually add the eggs, ground almonds, and orange-flower water or vanilla, if using, and beat until smooth.

3 Arrange the pears in a 10 in/25 cm flan dish. Sprinkle over ¹/₂ the raspberries and top with the egg mixture, smoothing with the back of a spoon. Bake for 25–30 minutes, until firm to the touch.

4 Meanwhile, put the reserved liquid into a small saucepan and bring to the boil. Boil for 5 minutes or until reduced to about 3 tablespoons. Increase the oven temperature to 450°F/230°C/Gas Mark 8. Spoon the liquid over the flan and bake for 5 minutes longer or until golden. Cool slightly, then decorate with the remaining raspberries and dust with the confectioners' sugar.

Serves 5

Plum Crumble

Ingredients

4 oz/115 g all-purpose flour

1 tsp apple spice

2 oz/55 g butter, chilled and diced

¼ cup superfine sugar

1 lb/455 g plums, halved and stoned

custard to serve

Method

1 Preheat the oven to 350°F/180°C/Gas Mark 4. Mix together the flour and apple spice in a bowl. Add the butter and, using your fingertips, rub it into the flour until the mixture resembles fine breadcrumbs. Stir in 1 oz/30 g of the sugar.

2 In another bowl, mix together the remaining sugar and the plums. If the fruit tastes particularly sour, add a little more sugar to taste. Arrange the fruit in a 9 x 6 in/23 x 15 cm ovenproof dish and spoon the crumble mixture evenly over the top.

3 Bake for 45–50 minutes, until the fruit is soft when pierced with a knife and the crumble topping is crisp and golden. Serve with the custard.

Serves 4

Prune Batter Pudding

Ingredients

1 1/4 cups milk

2 eggs

1 cup all-purpose flour

1/2 cup superfine sugar,
   plus extra to sprinkle

2 oz/55 g butter

1 cup pitted large dessert prunes

2 tbsp brandy

cream to serve

Method

1 Make a smooth batter of the milk, eggs, flour, and 1/2 the sugar. Add 1/2 the butter, melting it first, and mix at low speed with a food processor, electric blender, or beat well with a balloon whisk. Set aside to stand for 1 hour or so in the refrigerator.

2 Meanwhile, macerate the prunes in the brandy. Use the remaining butter to spread in a 9 1/2 in/24 cm shallow ovenproof dish. Sprinkle the prunes with the remaining sugar and brandy, spreading over the pie plate. Pour the batter over the prunes.

3 Bake in a preheated hot oven 400°F/200°C/Gas Mark 6 for about 30 minutes, reducing heat to moderately slow for the last 10 minutes if necessary to prevent too much browning. Serve at once, sprinkled with the extra superfine sugar and accompanied by the cream.

Serves 4

Risotto of Caramelized Apples and Pears

Ingredients

3 tbsp butter

3 tbsp sugar

2 tbsp maple syrup

2 Golden Delicious apples

1 Beurre Bosc pear

1 tsp cinnamon

2¹/₃ cups apple juice

1¹/₄ cups water

1 tbsp butter

14 oz/400 g arborio rice

¹/₃ cup white wine

4 tbsp sour cream

¹/₂ tsp cinnamon

**1 red apple, coarse grated and
   tossed with lemon juice**

Method

1 In a non stick frying pan, heat the butter, sugar, and maple syrup, and boil until syrupy, about 3 minutes.

2 Add the peeled, cored, and sliced fruit and cinnamon, and toss in the butter mixture. Simmer the fruit until caramelized and golden, about 10–15 minutes. Set aside.

3 Mix the apple juice and water together and heat to simmering.

4 In a saucepan, melt the butter and add the rice, stirring to coat. Allow the rice to absorb the butter, then add the wine, simmering until the alcohol has evaporated and the rice is dry.

5 Begin to add the simmering apple water, 1 cup at a time, stirring well after each addition and allowing the liquid to be absorbed before adding more apple water.

6 When ¹/₂ the apple water has been absorbed, add the caramelized apples and pears, and stir well to distribute.

7 Continue adding the apple water as before until it has all been absorbed.

8 Remove the pan from the heat and add ¹/₂ the sour cream. Stir well to distribute.

9 Serve in individual bowls, garnished with a small dollop of sour cream, a sprinkling of cinnamon, and some of the grated apple.

Serves 4

211

Strasbourg Apple Pie

Ingredients

Pastry

1 cup all-purpose flour

pinch of salt

2 oz/55 g butter

2 tbsp superfine sugar

1 egg

a few drops of vanilla extract

Filling

3 Golden Delicious or
   Granny Smith apples

$1/2$ cup sugar

1 tsp ground cinnamon

3 egg yolks

$1/2$ cup cream

Method

1 To make the pastry, sift the flour with a pinch of salt on to a pastry board. Make a well in the center and add the butter, sugar, egg and vanilla. Work at the ingredients in the center with your fingertips. When it is well mixed, gradually draw in the surrounding flour, then knead lightly to form a smooth dough. Wrap and chill for at least 1 hour.

2 Roll the dough out to fit a 8 in/20 cm flan ring or pie dish. Prick the base with a fork and chill a further 15 minutes.

3 To prepare the filling now, peel and core the apples and cut into quarters. Cut each $1/4$ into thin slices and arrange in the pastry shell. Sprinkle with $1/2$ the sugar and the cinnamon, and bake for about 30 minutes in a moderate oven at 350°F/180°C/Gas Mark 4.

4 Meanwhile, beat the egg yolks with the remaining sugar and cream and pour over the apples. Return to the oven and bake for a further 10–15 minutes until set and golden brown. Serve warm or cold.

Serves 4–6

Sweet Potato Tart

Ingredients

unsaturated oil for greasing

¹/₂ quantity Sweet Almond Pastry

Sweet Potato Filling

**14 oz/400 g red sweet potato
   scrubbed**

¹/₄ cup maple syrup

I egg

3 egg whites

**¹/₂ cup low-fat fruit yogurt
   of your choice (peach, apricot,
   or passionfruit are all delicious
   choices)**

I tsp ground ginger

I tsp ground cinnamon

¹/₂ tsp ground nutmeg

¹/₂ tsp ground allspice

Sweet Almond Pastry

I¹/₂ cup all-purpose flour

¹/₂ tsp baking powder

¹/₂ cup ground almonds

I tbsp wheatgerm

I tbsp cornstarch

I tbsp sugar

**I¹/₂ tbsp unsaturated
   margarine**

¹/₃ cup chilled skim milk

¹/₄ cup cold water, optional

Method

1 Preheat the oven to 350°F/180°C/Gas Mark 4. Lightly spray or brush a 9 in/23 cm pie dish with the unsaturated oil.

2 Roll out the pastry. Line the pie dish. Crimp the edges and prick the base a few times with a fork. Cover with plastic wrap. Chill until ready to use.

3 To make the filling, roast the sweet potato in its skin for 40 minutes or until soft. Peel. Press flesh through a sieve to remove any hard fibrous pieces. There should be a good I ¹/₂ cups of flesh.

4 Place the sweet potato, maple syrup, egg, egg whites, yogurt, ginger, cinnamon, nutmeg, and allspice in a food processor. Purée. Pour the mixture into the prepared pastry case. Bake for 40 minutes or until set – a knife inserted in the center should come out clean.

5 To make the pastry, place the flours, almonds, wheatgerm, cornstarch, and sugar in a food processor. Using the pulse button, process until just combined. Add the margarine. Using the pulse button, process until the mixture resembles fine breadcrumbs. With machine running, slowly add the milk until the mixture forms a ball. If necessary add the cold water. Turn the pastry onto a lightly floured surface. Knead briefly, until the pastry is smooth. Wrap in plastic wrap. Refrigerate for at least 30 minutes or until ready to use.

Serves 12 slices

215

Treacle Tart

Ingredients

9 oz/255 g shortcrust pastry,
   defrosted if frozen

16 oz/455 g can corn syrup

¹/₂ cup fresh white breadcrumbs

1 tsp ground ginger

finely grated rind of 1 lemon and
   juice of ¹/₂ lemon

2 eating apples, peeled, cored, and
   coarsely grated

Method

1 Preheat the oven to 375°F/190°C/Gas Mark 5. Roll out the pastry on a lightly floured surface and use to line a 8 in/20 cm flan tin at least 1 in/2¹/₂ cm deep. Trim off the excess pastry and reserve for decoration. Line with baking paper and baking beans, then bake blind for 10–12 minutes, until the pastry is lightly golden. Remove the paper and beans.

2 Meanwhile, make the filling. Open the can of syrup and place in a saucepan. Pour in boiling water to reach halfway up the tin. Warm over a low heat for 5 minutes or until the syrup is very runny. Place the breadcrumbs, ginger, lemon rind and juice, and apples in a bowl. Pour over the syrup and mix.

3 Pour the mixture into the pastry case. Roll out the reserved pastry and cut into strips, then twist gently. Lay the strips in a criss-cross pattern on top of the tart. Bake for 25–30 minutes, until bubbling.

Serves 4

Warm Plum Flan

Ingredients

Pastry

cream, softly whipped, to serve

1 cup all-purpose flour

1/2 cup cornstarch

3 oz/85 g butter

1 tsp superfine sugar

1 egg yolk

a few drops vanilla extract

Filling

1 lb/455 g plums

1/2 cup sugar

1/4 cup water

2 tsp extra cornstarch

1 tsp lemon juice

1/4 cup flaked almonds

Method

1 First make the pastry. Sift the flour and cornstarch together into a bowl. Rub in the butter, then stir in the sugar. Mix to a dough with the egg yolk lightly beaten with a teaspoon of water and the vanilla extract. Knead lightly, wrap, and chill for 30 minutes or so. Roll out and use to line a 8 in/20 cm flan ring. Trim, prick the base then bake 'blind' (lined with greaseproof paper and quarter filled with dried beans) for 20 minutes in a hot oven at 400°F/200°C/Gas Mark 6. Remove paper and beans and bake a further 5 minutes. Leave to cool while preparing the filling.

2 Halve the plums, remove the stones and poach in a syrup made up with 1/2 the sugar and the water, until just tender. Drain well and reserve the juice. Mix the extra cornstarch with the remaining sugar and a little of the reserved plum juice. Heat the rest of the juice in a small pan and pour in the cornstarch mixture, stirring all the time. Allow to boil until thickened, then stir in the lemon juice.

3 Brush the base of the pastry flan with this glaze and the arrange plums on top, rounded side up. Use the remaining glaze to brush over the plums, then arrange the almonds decoratively on top. Return the flan to the hot oven for a further 5–10 minutes, until the glaze has set, almonds have toasted and the pastry colored nicely. Serve warm with the softly whipped cream.

Serves 4

Cream Cheese and Apple Biscuits

Ingredients

**2 oz/55 g butter, cubed, plus extra
for greasing**

7 oz/200 g all-purpose flour

1 tsp baking powder

salt

**1/4 cup fine oatmeal, plus extra
for dusting**

1/2 tsp English mustard powder

1 tsp light muscovado sugar

**4 oz/115 g cream cheese,
cut into 1/2 in/1 cm cubes**

**1 large or 2 small eating apples,
peeled, cored, and chopped
into 1/4 in/5 mm pieces**

**4–5 tbsp soured cream
or buttermilk, plus extra
for glazing**

Method

1 Preheat the oven to 400°F/200°C/Gas Mark 6.
Grease a baking sheet.

2 Sift the flour, baking powder, and a good pinch of
salt into a bowl, then stir in the oatmeal, mustard
powder, and sugar. Rub in the butter using your
fingertips until it resembles fine breadcrumbs. Stir in
the cheese and apples and bind with just enough
soured cream or buttermilk to make a soft but not
sticky dough.

3 Roll out the dough on a floured surface to about
3/4 in/2 cm thick and stamp out 8 biscuits, using a
2 1/2 in/6 cm pastry cutter. Without overhandling the
dough, press the trimmings together, and roll out
again to make more biscuits. Place on the baking
sheet, brush the tops with soured cream or
buttermilk, and lightly dust with the extra oatmeal.
Bake for 15 minutes, then cool on a wire rack for a
few minutes before serving.

Makes 10–12 biscuits

In this section, you will find a magnificent array of tempting chocolate treats. Welcome to "Chocolate Heaven", where indulgence is the order of the day! Use these recipes to impress your friends and family with a truly stunning dessert.

Chocolate Heaven

Chocolate Heaven

Blueberry and Chocolate Soft-Bake Cookies

Ingredients

2 oz/55 g butter or margarine, cubed, plus extra for greasing

5 oz/145 g all-purpose flour

1¹/₂ tsp baking powder

1 tsp ground cinnamon

3 oz/85 g raw sugar

4 fl oz/115 mL whole milk

4 oz/115 g carton fresh blueberries

¹/₄ cup white chocolate chips

Method

1 Preheat the oven to 375°F/190°C/Gas Mark 5. Lightly grease a large baking sheet. Sift the flour, baking powder, and cinnamon into a bowl. Rub in the butter or margarine, using your fingertips, until the mixture resembles rough breadcrumbs, then stir in the sugar.

2 Stir in the milk, blueberries, and chocolate chips until just combined (the dough will be quite sticky). Spoon 8 mounds, spaced well apart, onto the baking sheet and cook for 20 minutes or until golden and springy to the touch. Cool on a wire rack for a few minutes before serving.

Serves 4

Hot Chocolate Soufflé

Ingredients

**1 oz/30 g sweet butter, plus
  extra for greasing**

**5 oz/145 g semisweet chocolate,
  broken into chunks**

6 large eggs, separated

3 oz/85 g superfine sugar

2 tbsp cornstarch

1 cup whole milk

confectioners' sugar to dust

Method

1 Place a baking sheet in the oven and preheat to 400°F/200°C/Gas Mark 6. Lightly butter a 6 cup soufflé dish. Melt the chocolate with the butter in a bowl placed over a saucepan of simmering water.

2 Whisk the egg yolks and sugar in a large bowl until pale and fluffy. Blend the cornstarch with 1 tablespoon of the milk. Heat the remaining milk in a pan, add the cornstarch mixture, and bring to the boil, stirring. Cook for 1 minute or until thickened. Remove from the heat and stir into the egg mixture with the melted chocolate, combining thoroughly.

3 Whisk the egg whites until they form stiff peaks (this is best done with an electric whisk). Fold a spoonful of egg white into the chocolate mixture to loosen, then gently fold in the rest. Spoon into the dish and place on the heated baking sheet. Cook for 35 minutes or until well risen. Dust with the confectoners' sugar and serve immediatey.

Serves 4

Ice Cream with Hot Chocolate Sauce

Ingredients

1 oz/30 g cocoa powder, sifted

1/2 cup soft light or dark brown sugar

1 oz/30 g butter

1 tbsp corn syrup

4 servings vanilla ice cream

Method

1 Place the cocoa powder and 1 cup boiling water in a small saucepan, stir to combine, then gently bring to the boil. Reduce the heat and simmer for 10 minutes or until reduced by about 3/4, whisking from time to time.

2 Stir in the sugar, butter, and corn syrup and cook gently for 2–3 minutes, until the sugar and butter have melted and the sauce looks shiny.

3 Put the ice cream into 4 bowls. Pour over the hot chocolate sauce and serve immediately.

Serves 4

Chocolate and Date-Stuffed Baklava

Ingredients

9 oz/255 g butter, plus extra for greasing

1 pack filo pastry, about 24 sheets

2 oz/55 g chocolate, extra, chopped

heavy cream, if desired

Syrup

1 cup white sugar

1/2 cup brown sugar

2/3 cup water

pinch of ground allspice

pinch of ground ginger

pinch of ground cloves

Filling

7 oz/200 g walnuts, toasted

3 1/2 oz/100 g almonds, toasted

6 oz/170 g bittersweet chocolate, chopped

6 oz/170 g dates, stones removed

2 tbsp sugar

1 tbsp cinnamon

1 egg, beaten

Serves 12–24

Method

1 Preheat the oven to 375°F/190°C/Gas Mark 5. Make the syrup. Bring all the syrup ingredients to a simmer in a small saucepan, stirring until the sugar dissolves. Continue simmering for 1 minute, then cool completely.

2 Next, make the filling. Combine the walnuts, almonds, chocolate, dates, sugar, and cinnamon in a food processor and process until roughly chopped. Do not over process. Transfer the mixture to a bowl and mix in the beaten egg.

3 Butter a 12 in/30 cm x 20 cm metal baking dish. Unwrap the filo pastry and place it on a flat work-surface under a damp cloth. Melt the butter. Place 1 sheet of pastry in front of you, then brush lightly with the butter, paying particular attention to the edges of the sheet of pastry. Place another sheet of pastry on top of the first, repeating the buttering. Repeat with 6 more sheets so that you have 8 in all. Fold this pastry stack in half to make it fit perfectly into the prepared baking tin, placing it in the tin neatly. Sprinkle 1/2 the prepared nut filling over the pastry, taking care to make sure the coverage is even.

4 Repeat the buttering and folding with 8 more sheets of pastry and place the folded pastry over the nuts. Add the remaining nut filling over the second stack of pastry. Repeat the buttering and folding with the remaining sheets of pastry and place over the nuts.

5 Using a sharp knife, score the pastry into 4 long strips, then cut these strips diagonally to form 24 diamond-shaped pieces of baklava. Pour any remaining butter over the pastry, then bake for 40 minutes, until the top of the pastry is deep golden-brown. Pour the syrup over the baklava, then allow to cool completely.

6 Grate the remaining chocolate over the baklava, then allow to stand at room temperature overnight.

Chocolate Crème Brûlée with a Fruity Surprise

Ingredients

1 lb/455 g plum pudding, purchased

4¹/₃ cups fresh cream

¹/₂ cup superfine sugar

9 oz/255 g bittersweet chocolate

8 large egg yolks

1 tbsp Dutch cocoa

¹/₄ cup confectioners' sugar

Method

1 Preheat the oven to 300°F/150°C/Gas Mark 2.

2 Cut the plum pudding into tiny cubes and sprinkle the pudding cubes equally among the bases of each of 12 ovenproof ramekins.

3 Place a large stainless steel bowl over a pot of simmering water and whisk the cream and sugar together gently over the simmering water until the sugar has dissolved. Add the chocolate, broken into small pieces, and continue mixing until the chocolate has dissolved. Remove from the heat.

4 In a separate bowl, whisk the egg yolks until they form a smooth 'ribbon'. Mix the whisked egg yolks, chocolate mixture, and Dutch cocoa until thoroughly combined. Pour this custard mixture into a jug and divide between the prepared ramekins.

5 Place the ramekins into a large ovenproof baking dish and add hot water to reach halfway up the outsides. Bake for 30 minutes or until set. Remove the baking dish and take the ramekins out of the water bath. Chill the custards for at least 2 hours or overnight.

6 Before serving, sieve the confectioners' sugar generously over the custards. Caramelize the sugar under a broiler until bubbling and golden. Alternatively, for a bit of fun, purchase a small blow-torch from a good kitchenware shop and use this to caramelize the sugar. If broiling, watch carefully to avoid burning the sugar.

Serves 10–12

Chocolate Hazelnut Torte

Ingredients

9 oz/255 g bittersweet chocolate, broken into pieces

6 eggs, separated

1 cup sugar

10 oz/285 g hazelnuts, toasted and roughly chopped, plus extra to serve

1 tbsp rum

confectioners' sugar, sifted

cream to serve

Method

1 Place the chocolate in a heatproof bowl set over a saucepan of simmering water and heat, stirring, until the chocolate melts. Remove the bowl from the pan and let cool slightly.

2 Place the egg yolks and sugar in a bowl and beat until thick and pale. Fold the chocolate, hazelnuts, and rum into the egg mixture.

3 Place the egg whites into a clean bowl and beat until stiff peaks form. Fold the egg whites into the chocolate mixture. Pour the mixture into a greased and lined 9 in/23 cm springform tin and bake at 375°F/190°C/Gas Mark 5 for 50 minutes or until cake is cooked when tested with a skewer. Cool the cake in the tin. Dust the cake with the confectioners' sugar just prior to serving with the cream sprinkled with the extra hazelnuts.

Serves 8

Chocolate Ice Cream

Ingredients

1 cup superfine sugar

9 egg yolks

¹/₂ cup cocoa powder, sifted

2 cups milk

2¹/₂ cups thickened
** double cream**

¹/₂ cup melted milk chocolate

Method

1 Place the sugar and egg yolks in a bowl and beat until thick and pale.

2 Place the cocoa powder in a saucepan. Gradually stir in the milk and cream and heat over a medium heat, stirring constantly, until the mixture is almost boiling. Stir in the chocolate.

3 Remove the pan from the heat and whisk the hot milk mixture into the egg mixture. Set aside to cool.

4 Pour the mixture into a freezerproof container and freeze for 30 minutes or until the mixture begins to freeze around the edges. Beat the mixture until even in texture. Return to the freezer and repeat the beating process 2 more times. Freeze until solid. Alternatively, place the mixture in an ice-cream maker and freeze according to the manufacturer's instructions.

Serves 8

Chocolate Mascarpone Roulade

Ingredients

6 oz/170 g bittersweet chocolate

1/4 cup strong black coffee

5 eggs, separated

1/2 cup superfine sugar, plus extra for sprinkling

2 tbsp all-purpose flour, sifted

frosted rose petals

Mascarpone Filling

12 oz/340 g mascarpone

2 tbsp confectioners' sugar

2 tbsp brandy

1/2 cup chocolate-hazelnut spread

Method

1 Place the chocolate and coffee in a heatproof bowl set over a saucepan of simmering water and heat, stirring, until the mixture is smooth. Cool slightly.

2 Beat the egg yolks until thick and pale. Gradually beat in the sugar. Fold the chocolate mixture and flour into the egg yolks.

3 Beat the egg whites until stiff peaks form. Fold into the chocolate mixture. Pour the mixture into a greased and lined 10 1/2 in × 12 3/4 in/26 cm × 32 cm Swiss roll tin and bake for 20 minutes or until firm. Cool in the tin.

4 To make the filling, beat the mascarpone, confectioners' sugar and brandy in a bowl.

5 Turn the roulade onto a clean kitchen towel sprinkled with the extra sugar. Spread with the chocolate-hazelnut spread and 1/2 the filling and roll up. Spread with the remaining filling and decorate with the frosted rose petals.

Serves 8–10

Chocolate Pecan Gâteau

Ingredients

4 eggs, separated

³/₄ cup superfine sugar

2 tbsp brandy

7 oz/200 g pecans, roughly chopped

2 tbsp all-purpose flour

Chocolate-Brandy Glaze

10 oz/285 g milk chocolate

2 tsp instant coffee powder

¹/₃ cup thickened double cream

1 tbsp brandy

5 oz/145 g pecans, roughly chopped

Method

1 Place the egg yolks, sugar, and brandy in a bowl and beat until thick and pale. Place the egg whites in a clean bowl and beat until stiff peaks form. Fold the egg whites, pecans, and flour into the egg yolk mixture.

2 Pour the mixture into a lightly greased and lined 9 in/23 cm springform tin and bake at 325°F/160°C/Gas Mark 3 for 40 minutes or until the cake is firm. Cool in the tin.

3 To make the glaze, place the chocolate, coffee powder, cream, and brandy in a heatproof bowl set over a saucepan of simmering water and heat, stirring, until the mixture is smooth. Remove the bowl from the pan and set aside to cool slightly. Spread the glaze over the top and sides of the cooled cake. Sprinkle the pecans over the top of the cake and press into side of the cake. Allow to set before serving.

Serves 8

Chocolate Pound Cake

Ingredients

6 oz/170 g butter, softened

1½ cups superfine sugar

3 tsp vanilla extract

3 eggs, lightly beaten

3 cups all-purpose flour

1½ cups tsp baking powder

½ cup cocoa powder

1¼ cups milk

Method

1 Place the butter, sugar, and vanilla extract in a bowl and beat until light and fluffy. Gradually beat in the eggs.

2 Sift together the flour, baking powder, and cocoa powder. Fold the flour mixture and milk, alternately, into the butter mixture.

3 Pour the mixture into a greased and lined 8 in/20 cm square cake tin and bake at 375°F/190°C/Gas Mark 5 for 55 minutes or until the cake is cooked when tested with a skewer. Stand the cake in the tin for 10 minutes before turning onto a wire rack to cool.

Note: This rich buttery cake can be served plain, with a readymade chocolate sauce or with cream. A simple glacé icing drizzled over the top makes another delicious alternative.

Serves 10–12

Chocolate Profiteroles

Ingredients

6 oz/170 g bittersweet chocolate, melted

Choux Pastry

1 cup water

3 oz/85 g butter

1 cup all purpose flour

3 eggs

Chocolate Liqueur Filling

1/2 cup sugar

3 egg yolks

2 tbsp flour

1 cup milk

2 oz/55 g bittersweet chocolate, broken into pieces

1 tbsp orange-flavored liqueur

Method

1 To make the pastry, place the water and butter in a saucepan and slowly bring to the boil. As soon as the mixture boils, quickly stir in the flour, using a wooden spoon. Cook over a low heat, stirring constantly, for 2 minutes or until the mixture is smooth and leaves the sides of the pan.

2 Beat in the eggs 1 at a time, beating well after each addition and until the mixture is light and glossy.

3 Place heaped tablespoons of the mixture on greased baking trays and bake at 200°F/200°C/Gas Mark 6 for 10 minutes. Reduce oven temperature to 350°F/180°C/Gas Mark 4 and cook for 10 minutes longer or until the pastries are golden and crisp. Pierce a small hole in the base of each pastry and transfer to wire racks to cool.

4 To make the filling, place the sugar and egg yolks in a bowl and beat until thick and pale. Add the flour and beat until combined.

5 Place the milk, chocolate, and liqueur in a saucepan and heat over a medium heat, stirring constantly, until the mixture is smooth. Remove the pan from the heat and slowly stir in egg-yolk mixture. Return pan to heat and cook over medium heat, stirring constantly, until mixture thickens. Remove pan from heat, cover, and set aside to cool.

6 Place the filling in a piping bag fitted with a small, plain nozzle and pipe the filling through a hole in the base of the profiteroles. Dip the tops of the profiteroles in the melted chocolate and place on a wire rack to set.

Note: Serve with whipped cream and fresh fruit. The pastry puffs can be baked in advance, cooled completely, and stored in an airtight container at room temperature overnight or, for longer storage, in the freezer for up to 6 weeks before filling.

Serves 6–8

Chocolate Sand Cake

Ingredients

¹/₄ **cup sweet cookie crumbs**

**7 oz/200 g butter or margarine,
  plus extra for greasing**

6 eggs

¹/₂ **cup sugar**

¹/₂ **cup brown sugar**

2 cups all-purpose flour

1 tbsp baking powder

3 tbsp cocoa

¹/₃ **cup milk**

1 tsp vanilla extract

**1 cup mixed dried fruit (or 1 cup of
  any single variety of dried fruit, such
  as golden raisins or confectioners'
  sugar or cocoa powder to dust**

Method

1 Generously butter a non stick fluted cake tin and sprinkle the cookie crumbs all over the buttered area. Set aside. Preheat the oven to 335°F/170°C/Gas Mark 5.

2 Slowly melt the butter or margarine. Meanwhile, using an electric mixer, beat the eggs and sugars together until the mixture is very thick and pale, about 8 minutes. With the motor still running, add the melted butter to the egg mixture in a thin stream and continue beating until all the ingredients are combined.

3 In a separate bowl, mix the flour, baking powder, and cocoa together.

4 Combine the egg mixture, the flour mixture, the vanilla extract, and the milk with a wooden spoon, continuing to mix until the batter is smooth. Add the dried fruit and mix briefly to distribute.

5 Pour the batter into the prepared tin, then bake the cake at for 40 minutes. Allow to cool for a few minutes in the tin, then turn out onto a wire rack and cool.

6 Dust with a little confectioners' sugar or cocoa powder if desired.

Serves 10–12

246

Chocolate Self-Saucing Pudding

Ingredients

1 cup all-purpose flour

1 tsp baking powder

¼ cup cocoa powder

¾ cup superfine sugar

½ cup milk

1½ oz/45 g butter, melted

vanilla or chocolate ice
**   cream to serve**

Chocolate Sauce

¾ cup brown sugar

¼ cup powder, sifted

1¼ cups hot water

Method

1 Sift together the flour and cocoa powder in a bowl. Add the sugar and mix to combine. Make a well in the center of the dry ingredients, add the milk and butter, and mix well to combine. Pour the mixture into a greased 4-cup capacity ovenproof dish.

2 To make the sauce, place the brown sugar and cocoa powder in a bowl. Gradually add the water and mix until smooth. Carefully pour the sauce over the mixture in the dish and bake for 40 minutes or until the cake is cooked when tested with a skewer.

3 Serve scoops of the pudding with some of the sauce from the base of the dish and top with a scoop of vanilla or chocolate ice cream.

Serves 6

Grandma's Chocolate Cake

Ingredients

4 oz/115 g butter, softened

2 cups superfine sugar

2 eggs

2 tsp vanilla extract

1 cup all-purpose flour

1 tsp baking powder

³/₄ cup all-purpose flour

³/₄ cup cocoa powder

1 cup buttermilk

³/₄ cup raspberry jelly

Chocolate Sour-Cream Filling

**6 oz/170 g bittersweet chocolate,
   broken into pieces**

4 oz/115 g butter, chopped

3¹/₄ cups confectioners' sugar, sifted

¹/₂ cup sour cream

Method

1 Place the butter, sugar, eggs, and vanilla extract in a bowl and beat until light and fluffy. Sift together the flours, baking powder, and cocoa powder.

2 Fold the flour mixture and milk, alternately, into the butter mixture. Divide the mixture between 4 greased and lined 9 in/2 cm round cake tins and bake at 350°F/180°C/Gas Mark 4 for 25 minutes or until the cakes are cooked when tested with a skewer. Turn the cakes onto wire racks to cool.

3 To make the filling, place the chocolate and butter in a heatproof bowl set over a saucepan of simmering water, and heat, stirring, until the mixture is smooth. Remove the bowl from the pan. Add the confectioners' sugar and sour cream and mix until smooth.

4 To assemble the cake, place 1 cake on a serving plate, spread with some of the jelly and top with some filling. Top with a second cake, some of the more jam and filling. Repeat the layers to use all cakes and jelly. Finish with a layer of cake and spread the remaining filling over the top and sides of the cake.

Serves 8–10

New York Chocolate Cake

Ingredients

1 lb/455 g dark or bittersweet chocolate

1 lb/455 g butter

1 cup 'espresso' or other very strong coffee

1 cup packed brown sugar

8 large eggs

2¼ lb/1 kg frozen raspberries, thawed

juice of 1 lemon

2 tbsp sugar

2 cartons fresh raspberries to serve

Method

1 Preheat the oven to 350°F/180°C/Gas Mark 4 and butter a 9½ in/24 cm non stick cake tin or long non stick loaf tin (not a springform).

2 Chop the chocolate and place in a large heatproof bowl.

3 In a small saucepan, bring the butter, espresso, and sugar to the boil and simmer briefly. Pour the liquid over the chopped chocolate and allow to sit for a few minutes. Stir the ingredients gently to help the chocolate melt. Beat the eggs, then add to the chocolate mixture, whisking thoroughly.

4 Pour the batter into the prepared cake tin, then place the tin in a large roasting pan or baking dish. Pour in hot, not boiling, water to reach halfway up the sides of the cake tin, then bake for 1 hour. Remove the cake from the water bath and chill overnight.

5 The next day, remove the cake from the tin. If you find this difficult, fill the kitchen sink with some boiling water and dip the cake tin base in the water for a few seconds to loosen. Run a knife around the tin, then invert the cake onto a platter.

6 To make the raspberry sauce, purée the thawed berries and their juice with the lemon juice and sugar. Pour the sauce through a sieve, then chill for up to 2 days. Although it will not taste sweet, the acidity will be a perfect foil for the cake. Serve the cake with the raspberry sauce and the fresh raspberries. You may like a little fresh cream on the side.

Serves 10–12

Raspberry and White Chocolate-Filled Warm Mini Chocolate Cakes

Ingredients

Cake

9 oz/255 g butter, plus extra for greasing

1 tsp instant coffee granules

1½ cups hot water

7 oz/200 g cooking chocolate

2 cups superfine sugar

1½ cups all-purpose flour

1½ tsp baking powder

¼ cup Dutch cocoa

2 eggs

2 tsp vanilla extract

3 oz/85 g white chocolate (chopped finely)

3½ oz/100g raspberries, plus extra to serve

Sauce

1 cup cream

1 cup quality chocolate

2 tbsp Kahlua coffee liqueur

Method

1 Preheat the oven to 300°F/150°C/Gas Mark 2. In a small saucepan, melt the butter, coffee granules, and hot water together until smooth and then remove from the heat.

2 Add the cooking chocolate and sugar, and stir thoroughly until the chocolate has dissolved. Sift together the flour and cocoa, then add to the liquid chocolate mixture, and mix well. Whisk the eggs and vanilla, then add to the chocolate mixture.

3 Prepare 10–12 muffin cups (or 2 trays of 6 cups each) by lightly buttering them, then dusting lightly with flour. Tip out the excess. Place 2 tablespoons of the batter into each of the muffin cups, then add a spoonful of white chocolate and some raspberries to the center of each muffin cup. Divide the remaining chocolate batter between the muffin cups and tap gently to settle the mixture.

4 Bake at for 20 minutes or until firm on top when touched. When baked, remove the cakes from the oven and allow to cool in the tin for 5 minutes. Then carefully loosen each little cake from the tin. Turn the muffin tray upside down on a flat tray to remove.

5 Meanwhile, make the sauce. Heat the cream until boiling, then pour it over the chocolate pieces that have been broken up and placed in a heatproof bowl. Allow the cream and chocolate to sit for 10 minutes, then gently but thoroughly stir the mixture. Add the coffee liqueur and stir again until smooth.

6 To serve, drizzle the chocolate sauce over the plate, then carefully place each cake in the center of the plates with a few of the extra raspberries.

Serves 10

Raspberry Choc Truffle Cakes

Ingredients

¹/₂ cup cocoa powder, sifted

1 cup boiling water

4 oz/115 g butter

1³/₄ cups superfine sugar

1¹/₂ tbsp raspberry jelly

2 eggs

1²/₃ cups/all-purpose flour, plus
   1²/₃ tsp baking sifted

14 oz/400 g dark chocolate, melted

raspberries to serve

Raspberry Cream

4 oz/115 g raspberries, puréed
   and sieved

¹/₂ cup heavy double, whipped

Chocolate Sauce

4 oz/115 g dark chocolate

¹/₂ cup water

¹/₄ cup superfine sugar

1 tsp brandy, optional

Method

1 Combine the cocoa powder and boiling water. Mix to dissolve and set aside to cool.

2 Place the butter, sugar and jelly in a bowl and beat until light and fluffy. Beat in the eggs 1 at a time, adding a little flour and baking powder with each egg. Fold the remaining flour and cocoa mixture, alternately, into the creamed mixture.

3 Spoon the mixture into 8 lightly greased ¹/₂ cup capacity ramekins or large muffin tins. Bake at 350°F/180°C/Gas Mark 4 for 20-25 minutes or until cakes are cooked when tested with a skewer. Cool for 5 minutes, then turn onto wire racks to cool. Turn the cakes upside down and scoop out the center, leaving a ¹/₂ in/1 cm shell. Spread each cake with the melted chocolate to cover the top and sides, then place right way up on a wire rack.

4 To make the raspberry cream, fold the raspberry purée into the cream. Spoon the cream into a piping bag fitted with a large nozzle. Carefully turn the cakes upside down and pipe in the cream to fill the cavity. Place right way up on individual serving plates.

5 To make the sauce, place the chocolate and water in a small saucepan and cook over a low heat for 4–5 minutes or until the chocolate melts. Add the sugar and continue cooking, stirring constantly, until the sugar dissolves. Bring just to the boil, then reduce the heat and simmer, stirring, for 2 minutes. Set aside to cool for 5 minutes, then stir the in brandy, if using. Cool the sauce to room temperature. To serve, decorate the plates with the sauce.

Serves 8

Chocolate Soufflé

Ingredients

9 oz/255 g bittersweet chocolate, broken into pieces

1 cup thickened heavy cream

6 eggs, separated

1 cup superfine sugar

¼ cup all purpose flour

confectioners' sugar, sifted optional

Method

1 Place the chocolate and ½ the cream in a heatproof bowl set over a saucepan of simmering water and heat, stirring constantly, until the mixture is smooth. Remove the bowl from the pan and set aside to cool slightly.

2 Place the egg yolks and the sugar in a clean bowl and beat until thick and pale. Gradually beat in the flour and remaining cream and beat until combined.

3 Transfer the egg yolk mixture to a saucepan and cook over a medium heat, stirring constantly, for 5 minutes or until the mixture thickens. Remove the pan from the heat and stir in the chocolate mixture.

4 Place the egg whites in a clean bowl and beat until stiff peaks form. Fold the egg whites into the chocolate mixture. Divide the mixture evenly between 6 buttered and sugared 1 cup capacity soufflé dishes and bake at 375°F/190°C/Gas Mark 5 for 25 minutes or until the soufflé sare puffed. Dust with the confectioners' sugar, if desired, and serve immediately.

Note: To prepare soufflé dishes, brush the interior of each with melted sweet butter, coating lightly and evenly, then sprinkle lightly with superfine sugar to coat.

Serves 6

The Best Chocolate Torte

Ingredients

5 oz/145 g dark chocolate,
  broken into pieces

1 cup brown sugar

¹/₂ cup heavy cream

2 egg yolks

7 oz/200 g butter, softened

1 cup sugar

1 tsp vanilla extract

2 eggs, lightly beaten

2 cups all-purpose flour

1 tsp baking powder

³/₄ cup milk

3 egg whites

Rich Chocolate Icing

³/₄ cup sugar

³/₄ cup water

6 egg yolks

7 oz/200 g bittersweet
  chocolate, melted

9 oz/255 g butter, chopped

Decorations

3 oz/85 g flaked almonds,
  toasted

chocolate-drizzled
  strawberries

Method

1 Place the chocolate, brown sugar, cream, and egg yolks in a heatproof bowl set over a saucepan of simmering water and cook, stirring constantly, until the mixture is smooth. Remove the bowl from the pan and set aside to cool slightly.

2 Place the butter, sugar, and vanilla extract in a bowl and beat until light and fluffy. Gradually beat in the eggs. Sift together the flour and baking powder over the butter mixture. Add chocolate mixture and the milk, and mix until well combined.

3 Place the egg whites in a clean bowl and beat until stiff peaks form. Fold the egg whites into the chocolate mixture. Pour the mixture into 2 greased and lined 9 in/23 cm round cake tins and bake at 350°F/180°C/Gas Mark 4 for 40 minutes or until cakes are cooked when tested with a skewer. Stand the cakes in the tins for 5 minutes before turning onto wire racks to cool.

4 To make the icing, place the sugar and water in saucepan and heat over a low heat, stirring constantly, until the sugar dissolves. Bring to the boil, then reduce the heat, and simmer for 4 minutes or until the mixture is syrupy.

5 Place the egg yolks in a bowl and beat until thick and pale. Gradually beat in the sugar syrup and melted chocolate. Then gradually beat in the butter and continue beating until the mixture is thick. Cover and refrigerate until the icing is of a spreadable consistency.

6 To assemble the torte, split each cake horizontally. Place 1 layer of cake on a serving plate and spread with the icing. Top with a second layer of cake and the icing. Repeat layers to use the remaining cake. Spread the top and sides of the cake with the remaining icing. Press the almonds into the sides of the torte and decorate the top with the chocolate-drizzled strawberries.

Serves 10–12

White Chocolate Yogurt Cake

Ingredients

5 oz/145 g white chocolate, broken into pieces plus extra, grated to serve

2 cups all purpose flour

2 tsp baking powder

1 cup superfine sugar

2 eggs, lightly beaten

7 oz/200 g plain yogurt

1½ oz/45 g butter, melted

White Chocolate Icing

3 oz/85 g white chocolate

1 tbsp heavy cream

Method

1 Place the chocolate in a heatproof bowl set over a saucepan of simmering water and heat, stirring, until smooth. Remove the bowl from the pan and cool slightly.

2 Place the flour, baking powder, sugar, eggs, yogurt, and butter in a bowl and beat for 5 minutes or until the mixture is smooth. Add the melted chocolate and mix well to combine.

3 Pour the mixture into a greased 9 in/23 cm ring tin and bake at 350°F/180°C/Gas Mark 4 for 50 minutes or until the cake is cooked when tested with a skewer. Stand the cake in the tin for 5 minutes before turning onto a wire rack to cool.

4 To make the icing, place the chocolate and cream in a heatproof bowl set over a saucepan of simmering water, and heat, stirring, until the mixture is smooth. Spread the icing over the top and sides of the cake and sprinkle with the extra grated white chocolate.

Serves 10–12

Choc-Meringue Cake

Ingredients

whipped cream to decorate

Hazelnut Meringue

5 oz/145 g hazelnuts, ground

2 tbsp corn starch

1¼ cups sugar

6 egg whites

Chocolate Filling

8 oz/225 g sweet butter

6 oz/170 g bittersweet chocolate, melted

3 tbsp superfine sugar

2 cups cream

2 tbsp brandy

½ cup hazelnuts, ground

Chocolate Topping

5 oz/145 g bittersweet chocolate

2 tsp vegetable oil

Method

1 To make the meringue, mix together the ground hazelnuts, corn starch and ¾ cup of the sugar. Beat the egg whites until soft peaks form, add the remaining sugar a little at a time, and beat until thick and glossy. Fold into the hazelnut mixture.

2 Mark 3 x 8 in-squares/20 cm on baking paper and place on baking trays. Place the meringue mixture in a piping bag fitted with a small plain nozzle and pipe the mixture to outline the squares, then fill the squares with piped lines of the mixture. Bake at 250°F/120°C/Gas Mark 1 for 40–50 minutes, or until crisp and dry.

3 To make the filling, beat the butter until soft. Add the chocolate, sugar, and cream, and beat until thick. Fold in the brandy and hazelnuts.

4 To make the topping, place the chocolate and oil in the top of a double saucepan and heat over simmering water, stirring until the chocolate melts and the mixture is smooth. Remove the top pan and set aside to cool.

5 To assemble the cake, place a layer of meringue on a serving plate and spread with ½ the filling. Top with another meringue layer and the remaining filling. Cut the remaining meringue into squares and position at angles on top of the cake. Drizzle with the topping and decorate with the cream.

Serves 10

Muddy Puddles

Ingredients

digestive cookies

3 oz/85 g butter

3 oz/85 g semisweet chocolate

2 tbsp corn syrup

1 medium egg, beaten

few drops of vanilla extract

1/2 oz/15 g white chocolate

Method

1 Put the cookies into a plastic bag, seal, then grind with a rolling pin. Melt 1 oz/30 g of the butter in a saucepan. Remove from the heat and mix in the cookies. Line a muffin tin with 4 paper muffin cases. Divide the cookie mixture between them, pressing over the base and sides of each case with the back of a teaspoon. Refrigerate for 20 minutes or until firm.

2 Preheat the oven to 350°F/180°C/Gas Mark 4. Meanwhile, put the remaining butter, chocolate, and syrup into a bowl set over a saucepan of simmering water. Heat gently, stirring, until melted. Remove from the heat and cool for 5 minutes. Whisk in the egg and vanilla extract.

3 Spoon the chocolate mixture over the cookie bases and bake for 20 minutes or until just firm. Leave to cool for 10 minutes. Meanwhile, melt the white chocolate in a bowl set over a pan of simmering water, then drizzle over the puddles.

Serves 4

Rich Chocolate Souffles

Ingredients

1 tbsp melted butter

3$\frac{1}{2}$ oz/100 g golden sugar, plus 1 tbsp
   for sprinkling

3$\frac{1}{2}$ oz/100 g pack bittersweet
   chocolate, broken into pieces

2 tbsp orange juice

2 medium eggs, separated

$\frac{1}{2}$ tsp finely grated orange rind

pinch of salt

cocoa powder for dusting, optional

Method

1 Grease the sides of 4 individual $\frac{1}{2}$-cup-capacity ramekin dishes, or ovenproof soufflé dishes, with the melted butter. Sprinkle the tablespoon of sugar equally between the dishes, dust the sides, and shake out any excess. Preheat the oven to 375°F/190°C Gas Mark 5 and place a baking sheet in the oven.

2 Heat the chocolate and orange juice in a bowl, over a pan of simmering water, until the chocolate has melted and the mixture is smooth. Remove from the heat and stir in the egg yolks with the orange rind and $\frac{1}{2}$ the sugar.

3 Whisk the egg whites in a large bowl with a pinch of salt until they form stiff peaks, then slowly whisk in the remaining sugar. Fold $\frac{1}{4}$ of the egg whites into the chocolate, then fold in the remaining egg whites. Spoon the mixture into the dishes and place in the oven on the hot baking sheet. Cook for 12–14 minutes, until well risen and just set. Dust with the cocoa powder, if using, and serve.

Serves 4

Simple Chocolate Cake

Ingredients

1 tbsp confectioners' sugar to dust

Cake

1 tsp sunflower oil for greasing

**4 oz/115 g all purpose flour, plus 2 tsp
for flouring**

1 tsp baking powder

1 oz/30 g cocoa powder

1/2 cup superfine sugar

2 large eggs, lightly beaten

4 oz/115 g soft margarine

3 tbsp milk

Filling

5 fl oz/145 mL carton double cream

2 tbsp raspberry jelly

Method

1 Preheat the oven to 350°F/180°C/Gas Mark 4.
Grease 2 x 7 in/18 cm sandwich tins with the oil,
using a pastry brush or a folded sheet of kitchen
paper. Add a teaspoon of flour to each tin, then tilt
the tin, and knock the sides so that the flour covers
the inside. Tip out any excess.

2 Sift the flour, baking powder, and cocoa powder
into a bowl, add the sugar, eggs, margarine, and milk.
Be a wooden spoon or an electric whisk until the
mixture is soft and smooth.

3 Using a large metal spoon, divide the mixture
between the 2 tins, spreading evenly. Bake for 25
minutes, until the tops are firm and springy. To check
the cakes are cooked, insert a knife or skewer into
the middle of 1 – it should come out clean. If the
knife is sticky, bake for 5 minutes more and test
again. Leave to cool in the tins for 10 minutes.

4 To remove each cake from its tin, loosen the sides
with a knife, then place a large plate over the top
and flip the cake over. Cool the cakes, right-side up,
on a wire rack.

5 For the filling, whisk the cream until it forms soft
peaks. Spread 1 cake with the raspberry jelly, and
top with the cream. Place the other cake on top. Just
before serving, place the confectioners' sugar in a
sieve and tap lightly to dust the cakes with sugar.

Serves 4

Sweet Little Bonfires

Ingredients

4 oz/115 g dried mixed fruit

¼ cup corn flakes

3⅓ oz/100 g shredded wheat, crushed (about 4 biscuits)

3½ oz/100 g candied cherries, chopped

6fl oz/170 mL condensed milk

5 oz/145 g dried coconut

5 oz/145 g milk chocolate

Method

1 Preheat the oven to 160°C/325°F/Gas Mark 3. Line 3 baking sheets with baking or rice paper. Combine the dried mixed fruit, corn flakes, shredded wheat, cherries, condensed milk, and coconut in a large bowl. Press the mixture into little mounds and place on the baking sheets, spacing them evenly. Bake for 15 minutes or until golden and crisp.

2 Meanwhile, melt the chocolate in a bowl placed over a saucepan of simmering water. Remove the 'bonfires' from the oven and leave for 2 minutes to cool slightly. Drizzle over the melted chocolate and cool for a further 1–2 minutes before serving.

Makes 36

In this section, you will find an outstanding collection of desserts for that "special occasion". Be it a party to celebrate an event, a romantic dinner for two, or a dinner for special friends, use these recipes to finish your occasion in style.

Special Occasions

Special Occasions

Tiramisu Ice Cream

Ingredients

1 oz/30 g superfine sugar

**3 tbsp hot espresso or other
very strong black coffee**

**15 oz/425 g carton ready-to-serve
custard**

9 oz/255 g tub mascarpone

**3½ oz/100 g cocoa amaretti biscuits,
roughly crumbled**

3 tbsp marsala

semisweet chocolate to decorate

Method

1 Mix the sugar and coffee together and stir until the sugar has dissolved. Whisk together the custard and mascarpone until smooth, then stir in the coffee mixture, mixing evenly.

2 Pour into a freezer container and freeze for 1 hour or until ice crystals begin to form. Whisk the mixture until smooth, then return to the freezer for 30 minutes.

3 Sprinkle the biscuits with the marsala and quickly stir into the half-frozen ice cream, mixing well. Return to the freezer for 1 hour or until firm. Serve the ice cream decorated with the curls of chocolate made with a vegetable peeler.

Serves 4

Pecan and Orange Tart

Ingredients

**7 oz/200 g unsweetened pastry,
defrosted if frozen**

1 large egg

5 tbsp maple syrup or clear honey

pinch of salt

1 tsp finely grated orange rind

¼ cup superfine sugar

2 oz/55 g butter, melted

½ cup pecan nuts

heavy cream, whipped, to serve

Method

1 Preheat the oven to 400°F/200°C/Gas Mark 6. Roll the pastry out thinly on a lightly floured surface and use it to line a 8 in/20 cm loose-bottomed flan tin. Refrigerate for 10 minutes.

2 Line the pastry with baking paper and baking beans. Cook for 15 minutes, then remove the paper and beans, and cook for another 5 minutes or until lightly golden. Cool for 5 minutes.

3 Whisk the egg with the maple syrup or honey, salt, orange rind, sugar, and butter until blended. Pour the mixture into the pastry case and arrange the pecan nuts on top. Bake for 30 minutes or until set. Cool in the tin for 15 minutes. Serve with whipped heavy cream.

Serves 4

Baked Apple Cheesecake

Ingredients

7 oz/200 g prepared
  unsweetened pastry
1 oz/30 g butter
2 apples, cored, peeled, and sliced
confectioners' sugar to serve

Ricotta Filling
1²/₃ lb/750 g ricotta cheese
4 eggs, separated
¹/₂ cup honey
1 tbsp finely grated orange rind
3 tbsp orange juice

Method

1 Roll out the pastry to ¹/₈ in/3 mm thick and use to line a deep 9 in/23 cm flan tin with a removable base. Prick the base and sides of the pastry with a fork, line with nonstick baking paper and fill with uncooked rice. Bake at 400°F/200°C/Gas Mark 6 for 10 minutes, then remove the rice and paper, and bake for 5–8 minutes longer or until lightly browned.

2 Melt the butter in a frying pan, add the apple slices, and cook over a medium heat, stirring occasionally, until golden. Set aside to cool. Arrange the apples evenly over the base of the pastry case.

3 To make the filling, place all the filling ingredients, except the egg whites, in a food processor and process until smooth.

4 Place the egg whites in a separate bowl and beat until stiff peaks form. Fold the egg white mixture into the ricotta mixture. Carefully pour the filling over the apples.

5 Reduce the oven temperature to 350°F/180°C/Gas Mark 4 and bake for 1¹/₄ hours or until firm. Set aside to cool, then refrigerate overnight. Serve dusted with the confectioners' sugar.

Serves 8

Banana and Honey Tea Bread

Ingredients

½ cup sunflower spread, plus extra
   for greasing
½ cup light soft brown sugar
½ cup set honey
2 medium eggs, beaten
1 cup all-purpose whole-wheat flour
1 tsp baking powder
1 tsp ground nutmeg
3 bananas
lemon juice

Method

1 Preheat the oven to 350°F/180°C/Gas Mark 4. Lightly grease and line a 2 lb/900 g loaf tin. Beat together the sunflower spread, sugar, and honey in a bowl until light and fluffy. Gradually beat in the eggs, then fold in the flour and nutmeg.

2 Mash the bananas with a little lemon juice and fold them into the mixture until thoroughly combined. Spoon the mixture into the prepared tin and level the surface with the back of a spoon.

3 Bake for 1–1¼ hours or until risen, golden, and firm to the touch. If necessary, cover lightly with baking paper or foil towards the end of the cooking to prevent the top of the bread overbrowning.

4 Cool for a few minutes in the tin, then turn out onto a wire rack and leave to cool completely.

Serves 4

Fresh Mango and Mascarpone Brûlée

Ingredients

4 large ripe mangoes
9 oz/255 g tub mascarpone
7 oz/200 g tub strained yogurt
1 1/2 tsp dried ground ginger
finely grated rind and juice of 1 lime
1 tbsp dark or light rum, optional
6 tbsp light muscovado sugar
2/3 oz/20 g sweet butter
fresh mint to decorate, optional

Method

1 Peel the mangoes, using a vegetable peeler, then slice the flesh off the stone, and chop, collecting any juices in a bowl.

2 Whisk together the mascarpone and yogurt using a whisk or a fork, then stir in the ginger, lime rind, and juice. Whisk in the rum, if using.

3 Place the mango and juices in a deep 7 in/18 cm ovenproof dish, or divide between 6 ovenproof ramekins. Spoon over the mascarpone mixture, then sprinkle over the sugar, and dot with the butter. Refrigerate until required.

4 Preheat the broiler to high. Broil the dessert for 4–5 minutes in the dish or 1–2 minutes in the ramekins, until lightly golden and bubbling. Cool for 1–2 minutes, then decorate with the mint, if using.

Serves 6

Oriental Fruit Salad

Ingredients

3 stalks lemongrass

2 oz/55 g superfine sugar

1 small cantaloupe melon

1 mango

15 oz/425 g can lychees, drained

fresh mint leaves to garnish

Method

1 Peel the outer layers from the lemongrass stalks, finely chop the lower white bulbous parts, and discard the fibrous tops. Place the lemongrass, sugar, and $1/2$ cup of water in a saucepan. Simmer, stirring, for 5 minutes or until the sugar dissolves, then bring to the boil. Remove from the heat and leave to cool for 20 minutes. Refrigerate for 30 minutes.

2 Halve the melon and scrape out the seeds. Cut into wedges, then remove the skin, and cut the flesh into small chunks. Slice off the 2 fat sides of the mango close to the stone. Cut a criss-cross pattern across the flesh (but not the skin) of each piece, then push the skin inside out to expose the cubes of flesh and cut them off.

3 Place the melon, mango, and lychees in serving bowls. Strain the lemongrass syrup and pour over the fruit. Decorate with the mint.

Serves 4

Strawberry and Cream Tartlets

Ingredients

5 oz/145 g all-purpose flour

**1 tbsp confectioners' sugar,
plus extra to dust**

**½ oz/100 g sweet butter,
softened**

**finely grated zest of 1 small
lemon, plus 1 tsp juice**

**5 fl oz/145 mL heavy or
whipping cream**

**8 oz/225 g strawberries,
halved**

**4 tbsp raspberry jelly or
redcurrant jelly to glaze**

Method

1 Preheat the oven to 375°F/190°C/Gas Mark 5. Sift the flour and sugar into a bowl. Rub in the butter and the lemon juice, and knead lightly until the mixture forms a smooth dough. Cover with plastic wrap and refrigerate for 15 minutes.

2 Roll the dough out thinly on a lightly floured surface, divide it into 4, and use it to line 4 x 3 in/7½ cm loose-bottomed tartlet tins. Line with baking paper and baking beans and bake for 15 minutes. Remove the paper and beans, and cook for another 3–5 minutes, until the pastry is golden. Leave to cool for 15 minutes, then remove from the tins.

3 Whip the cream with the lemon zest until it forms soft peaks. Spoon into the cases and top with the strawberries. Melt the jelly over a gentle heat with 1 tablespoon of water, then press through a sieve, and cool slightly. Spoon over the strawberries, then dust with the confectioners' sugar.

Serves 4

Poached Ricotta Pears

Ingredients

4 pears, cored, peeled, and halved

2 cups red wine

1 cup water

2 tbsp sugar

1 cinnamon stick

Prune and Ricotta Filling

¹/₄ cup pitted prunes, halved

2 tbsp port

**³/₄ cup reduced-fat fresh
  ricotta cheese**

¹/₂ tsp vanilla extract

1 tsp grated orange zest

1 tsp confectioners' sugar

Method

1 To make the filling, place the prunes and port in a saucepan. Bring to the boil. Remove the pan from the heat. Cool.

2 Place the ricotta cheese, vanilla extract, orange zest, and confectioners' sugar in a food processor. Process until light and fluffy. Fold in the prunes with 1–2 teaspoons of their liquid. Set aside.

3 Preheat the oven to 350°F/180°C/Gas Mark 4. Cut a sliver off the curved side of each pear so they sit flat. Place the pears in a deep-sided frying pan, cavity side up.

4 Combine the wine, water, and sugar. Pour over the pears to cover. Add the cinnamon stick. Cover. Bring to simmering. Simmer for 10–15 minutes or until the pears are just tender.

5 Using a slotted spoon, transfer the pears to a baking dish. Spoon the filling into the cavities. Bake for 10 minutes or until the filling is set.

6 Bring the liquid remaining in the frying pan to the boil. Boil until it reduces to a glaze consistency. Serve with the pears.

Serves 4

Rhubarb and Strawberry Crumble

Ingredients

1 lb/455 g rhubarb, cut into chunks

8 oz/225 g strawberries, hulled and halved

2 oz/55 g brown sugar

Topping

5 oz/145 g all-purpose flour

pinch of salt

2 oz/55 g superfine sugar

2¹/₂ oz/75 g sweet butter, cubed

2¹/₂ oz/75 g ground almonds

2 oz/55 g slivered or flaked almonds

Method

1 Preheat the oven to 350°F/180°C/Gas Mark 4. Mix together the rhubarb, strawberries, and sugar. Transfer to a 8 x 12 in/20 x 30 cm ovenproof dish.

2 To make the topping, sift the flour and salt into a bowl, then stir in the superfine sugar. Rub the butter into the mixture using your fingertips until it resembles fine breadcrumbs. Stir in the ground and slivered almonds, then sprinkle the mixture over the fruit.

3 Bake for 40–45 minutes, until the fruit juices are bubbling, and the topping is lightly browned.

Serves 4

Roasted Peaches with Raspberry Sauce

Ingredients

4 ripe peaches, halved and stoned

1 oz/30 g butter

4 tbsp sugar

2 tbsp clear honey

1 oz/30 g almonds, halved lengthways

Raspberry Sauce

4 oz/115 g punnet raspberries

1 oz/30 g golden sugar

4 tbsp orange juice

Method

1 To make the sauce, place the raspberries in a food processor with the sugar and orange juice and pulse to combine. Alternatively, crush the raspberries with a fork, add the sugar and orange juice, and mix well. Pass the mixture through a sieve to remove any pips and set aside.

2 Preheat the oven to 400°F/200°C/Gas Mark 6. Line an ovenproof dish with baking paper and place the peach halves on top. Dot with the butter, sprinkle with the sugar, and drizzle over the honey. Cook for 10 minutes, remove from the oven, sprinkle over the almonds, return to the oven, and cook for 10 minutes or until the peaches are soft.

3 To serve, place the peach halves on individual plates and serve with the Raspberry Sauce.

Serves 4

Rum and Lime Banana Fritters

Ingredients

4 bananas

juice of 1 lime

2 tsp superfine sugar

1 tbsp dark rum

oil for deep-frying

Batter

3 1/2 oz/100 g all-purpose flour

1/4 tsp baking powder

pinch of salt

2 tbsp sesame seeds

Method

1 Peel each banana and cut in 1/2 crossways, then slice lengthways to make quarters. Place the banana quarters, lime juice, sugar, and rum in a deep, non-metallic dish and mix gently. Cover and set aside for 30 minutes to marinate.

2 Meanwhile, make the batter. Sift the flour and salt into a mixing bowl. Pour in 1/2 cup of water and whisk to form a smooth, thick batter. Stir in the sesame seeds and set aside.

3 Heat 2 in/5 cm of the oil in a wok or a large, deep frying pan until smoking hot. Coat the banana pieces thoroughly in the batter. Fry for 5 minutes or until golden brown, then turn over, and cook for 2 minutes to brown the other side (you may have to cook them in batches). Drain on paper towels and serve immediately.

Serves 4

Sticky Rice Sandcastles

Ingredients

**1 oz/30 g butter, plus extra
for greasing**

3 oz/85 g short-grain or pudding rice

1 1/4 cups whole milk

grated rind of 1/2 lemon

3 oz/85 g superfine sugar

pinch of cinnamon

soft light brown sugar to decorate

Method

1 Lightly grease 2 x 3/4 cup moulds or ramekins. Put the rice in a saucepan and cover with 3/4 cup of water. Bring to the boil, then reduce the heat, and simmer, covered, for 4–5 minutes, until the water is absorbed.

2 Heat the milk in a saucepan. Add the milk to the rice with the butter, lemon rind, sugar, and cinnamon. Simmer, uncovered, over a low heat, stirring occasionally, for 40 minutes or until the mixture is thick and creamy.

3 Spoon the rice into the moulds or ramekins. Cool for 10 minutes, then refrigerate for 1 hour or until set. Preheat the broiler to medium. Run a knife around the edge of each pudding and turn out onto a baking sheet. Sprinkle the tops with a layer of the brown sugar and broil for 1 minute or until the sugar caramelizes. Serve on individual plates, with a sprinkling of the brown sugar for the sand.

Serves 2

Austrian Maple Spice Cake

Ingredients

Cake

3 cups all-purpose flour

3 tsp baking powder

2 tbsp cinnamon

1 tsp ground cloves

2 tsp ground ginger

2 tbsp Dutch cocoa

1 cup pure maple syrup

1/2 cup honey

1 1/2 cups superfine sugar

1 1/2 cups buttermilk

1 tsp pure vanilla extract

Glaze

7 oz/200 g cooking chocolate

2 tbsp butter

juice and rind of 1 small orange

**3 tbsp marmalade
  or apricot jelly**

4 tbsp sugar

2 tsp water

Method

1 Butter a nonstick 11½ or 11 in/28 cm or 26 cm springform tin and set aside. Preheat the oven to 350°F/180°C/Gas Mark 4.

2 In a large bowl, mix together the flour, cinnamon, ground cloves, ginger, and cocoa. In a separate bowl, whisk the maple syrup, honey, sugar, buttermilk, and vanilla. Gently but thoroughly combine the flour mixture and the syrup mixture.

3 Pour the batter into the prepared cake tin and bake at 335°F/170°C/Gas Mark 3 for 1 hour and 10 minutes, until the cake is 'springy' when pressed gently in the center. Remove the cake from the oven and cool thoroughly in the tin. When the cake is cold, remove it from the cake tin and set aside.

4 To make the glaze, melt the chocolate and butter, either in the microwave or in a bowl resting over a saucepan of simmering water. When melted, whisk in the orange juice thoroughly.

5 Meanwhile, warm the marmalade or jelly and gently spread it over the surface of the cake. Allow to cool. When the chocolate mixture is smooth, carefully pour it over the marmalade or jelly topped cake and spread to cover.

6 Cut the rind of the orange into fine strips or use a 'zester'. Heat the sugar and water together in a small saucepan and, when liquid, add the orange strips, and simmer for 5 minutes. Lift out the caramelized orange strips and allow to cool. (Discard the remaining syrup.)

7 Before serving, pile the caramelized orange strips in the center of the cake.

Serves 10–12

Baklava

Ingredients

7 oz/200 g sweet butter, melted

14 oz/400 g blanched roasted almonds, ground

1½ tsp cinnamon

½ cup superfine sugar

1½ lb/700 g filo pastry

Syrup

3 cups superfine sugar

1½ cups water

1 cinnamon stick

1 piece of orange or lemon rind

1 tbsp honey

Method

1 Melt the butter, and set aside. Mix the nuts in a bowl, and add the cinnamon and sugar.

2 Brush a baking tray 10 x 14 in/25 x 33 cm in size with the butter.

3 Place 1 sheet of filo on the bottom of a dish with the ends hanging over the sides. Brush with the melted butter and add another layer of filo. Repeat with 8 more filo sheets.

4 Sprinkle the nut mixture generously over the filo. Continue the layering of the filo pastry (3 sheets) and 1 layer of the nuts until all the nuts are used. Top with the 8 reserved sheets of the filo, making sure the top sheet is well buttered. Cut the top lengthways in parallel strips.

5 Bake in the oven at 475°F/275°C/Gas Mark 8 for 30 minutes, then reduce the heat to 325°F/150°C/Gas Mark 3 and bake for a further hour. Pour the cold syrup over the baklava and cut into diamond shapes.

6 To make the syrup, place all the ingredients in a saucepan and bring to the boil. Reduce the heat and let simmer for 10–15 minutes. Leave to cool before use.

Serves 10–12

Black Sesame Blancmanger

Ingredients

7 fl oz/200 mL milk

11 fl oz/310 mL heavy cream

2 1/2 tbsp sugar

1 tbsp gelatine powder

3 tsp amaretto

2 tbsp kuromerigoma*

2 tbsp shiromerigoma*

4 tbsp kuromitsu sauce*

Caramelized Filo

1 sheet filo pastry

sugar

white sesame seeds

* Available in Asian food stores

Method

1 To make the caramelized filo, place the filo pastry on a greased oven tray, lightly sprinkle with the sugar and place under a hot grill until the sugar caramelizes. Remove from the heat and immediately sprinkle with white sesame seeds. Allow to cool then break into pieces and set aside.

2 Place the milk, cream and sugar in a saucepan. Heat gently until sugar has dissolved. Remove from heat. Carefully sprinkle gelatine over and stir until dissolved. Stir in amaretto.

3 Divide the mixture into three equal parts. Stir the black sesame paste into one third.

Mix the white sesame paste into another third and leave the last plain.

4 Pour the black sesame blancmange into the base of four cold dessert glasses. Carefully pour the white sesame blancmange over this. Finally top with the plain blancmange. Refrigerate 1–2 hours until set.

5 Top each blancmange with 1 tablespoon kuromitsu sauce and some broken caramelized filo. Serve with some mixed berries.

Serves 4

Blueberries and Champagne Sabayon

Ingredients

15 oz/425 g can blueberries, drained, plus extra to serve

4 egg yolks

2 tbsp superfine sugar

1/2 cup champagne or sparkling white wine

homemade shortbread to serve

Method

1 Spoon the blueberries into individual serving dishes or glasses and refrigerate. Place the egg yolks, sugar, and champagne into the top of a double boiler and beat over a medium heat, until the mixture thickens and becomes light and fluffy.

2 Pour the sabayon over the blueberries, and serve at once with homemade shortbread.

Serves 4–6

Caramel Cherries

Ingredients

16 oz/455g canned, pitted sweet cherries, drained

1 1/4 cups heavy cream, whipped

1 tsp liqueur of your choice or sherry

brown sugar

Method

1   Place the cherries in a shallow ovenproof dish.

2   Place the cream and liqueur or sherry in a bowl and beat until soft peaks form. Spoon the cream mixture over the cherries, sprinkle thickly with the brown sugar, and cook under a preheated hot broiler for 3–4 minutes or until the sugar melts. Serve immediately.

Serves 6

Coconut Flan with Caramel (Créme Caramel)

Ingredients

Caramel

¹/₄ **cup sugar**

¹/₄ **cup hot water**

Custard

4 eggs

1 tsp vanilla extract

1 cup fresh, canned, or
   reconstituted powdered
   coconut milk

1 cup milk

¹/₄ **cup sugar**

mint sprig to decorate

Method

1 To make the caramel, melt the sugar alone in a small, heavy saucepan, over a low heat. Swirl the saucepan constantly until the sugar becomes golden. Stir in the hot water carefully as the mixture will splatter. Quickly stir to dissolve any lumps and boil for about 2 minutes until the liquid is clear.

2 Pour the caramel into a 4-cup-capacity soufflé dish that has been lightly greased with butter or margarine. Tilt the dish to ensure the caramel coats the base.

3 To make the custard, beat the eggs and vanilla in a large bowl. Combine the coconut milk and milk with the sugar in a saucepan and cook over low heat until the sugar dissolves. Remove from the stove and beat quickly into the eggs and vanilla so the eggs do not curdle. Sieve the custard only if it is lumpy. Pour slowly on top of the caramel in the soufflé dish.

4 Preheat the oven to 325°F/160°C/Gas Mark 3. In the base of a large roasting pan, place 2 layers of paper towelling, then place the soufflé dish on top before pouring hot water into the roasting pan until halfway up the soufflé dish. Bake in the center of the oven for about 50 minutes or until a knife inserted into the custard is clean when removed. Do not allow the water to boil. Remove the soufflé. Cool in a pan of cold water. Chill, covered with plastic wrap, preferably overnight.

5 To serve, run a knife around the circumference of the dish and place a dinner plate on top. In a quick movement, invert the dish and the créme caramel will slide onto the plate. Serve alone or with whipped cream. Place the mint sprig in the center to garnish.

Serves 6

Deep Fried Banana Wrapped In Filo

Ingredients

4 sheets filo pastry

4 bananas, peeled

1/2 cup ogura (red bean paste)

2 tsp yuzu peel*

oil for deep frying

confectioners' sugar

4 tbsp kuromitsu sauce*

* Available in Asian food stores

Method

1 Lay 1 piece of filo pastry onto a board. Place a whole banana near 1 corner. Spoon 2 tablespoons of the red bean paste and 1/2 teaspoon of the yuzu peel beside the banana. Roll up the pastry to fully enclose the banana, like a parcel.

2 Heat the oil to 350°F/180°C and deep-fry the banana parcel for 3–4 minutes, until golden. Repeat with remaining ingredients.

3 Cut the bananas in 1/2 diagonally, dust with the confectioners' sugar, and serve each with 1 tablespoon of the kuromitsu sauce.

Serves 4

English Syrup Sour Cream Cake

Ingredients

7 oz/200 g soft butter
  plus extra for greasing
7 oz/200 g superfine sugar
1 tsp vanilla extract
3 eggs
1 apple, peeled and grated
1 cup all-purpose flour
1 tsp baking powder
3½ oz/100 g sour cream
5 tbsp corn syrup
5 tbsp corn syrup, extra
fresh fruit and custard or cream
  to serve

Method

1 Preheat the oven to 375°F/190°C/Gas Mark 5 and grease an 8 in/20 cm cake tin (not springform). Line the base of the tin with baking paper, allowing the paper to come up the sides a little. Press the paper to the sides of the tin.

2 Cream the butter and sugar together, then add the vanilla and the eggs, 1 at a time, and beating well after each addition. Add the grated apple, then the sieved combined flour and baking powder, then the sour cream, beating well to combine all the ingredients thoroughly until the mixture is smooth.

3 Pour the corn syrup into the base of the prepared cake tin, then spoon the cake batter over the top.

4 Cover the cake tin with a large piece of buttered foil, buttered side down towards the cake batter, and secure the foil with string around the edge of the cake tin. Place the cake tin in a large baking dish and add hot water until it reaches halfway up the side of the cake tin.

5 Bake for 75 minutes, then remove the cake tin from the water and allow to cool for 20 minutes before turning out onto a cake platter.

6 Heat the extra corn syrup, then pour over the top of the cake, and serve with some fresh fruit of your choice, and some custard or cream.

Serves 8

Ginger Pears in a Puff Pastry Coat

Ingredients

2 cups sugar

4 cups red wine

1 cup Crème de Cassis

**2 oz/55 g piece ginger,
  peeled and sliced**

**8 firm brown cooking pears,
  stalks intact**

2 sheets puff pastry

1 egg white

1 tbsp sugar, extra

Method

1 Preheat the oven to 400°F/210°C/Gas Mark 6.

2 Preferably a day ahead, place the sugar, red wine, Crème de Cassis, and ginger in a large saucepan and heat gently. Meanwhile, peel all the pears, taking care to leave the stalks intact. Place each pear in the hot liquid and then bring to the boil. Reduce the heat to a simmer and cook the pears slowly for 30 minutes. Allow the pears to cool, then refrigerate them in their cooking liquid until ready to bake.

3 Lift the pears out of the poaching liquid, then simmer the poaching liquid for 20 minutes until it has reduced and is syrupy.

4 Cut each of the 2 pastry sheets into ¼ so that you now have 8 squares of pastry. Place a square of pastry over each pear, pushing gently so that the stalk of the pear protrudes through the pastry square. Pleat the sides of the pastry pieces so that they look attractive.

5 Whisk the egg white until frothy, then lightly brush the tops of each pastry square. Sprinkle with the extra tablespoon of sugar. Place the 'coated' pears in a shallow baking dish. Bake for 10 minutes or until the pastry is golden and crisp.

6 Serve each pear with a drizzle of the reduced pear syrup.

Serves 8

Greek Rum and Hazelnut Cake

Ingredients

Cake

1 lb/455 g toasted hazelnuts

3 1/2 oz/100 g plain sweet cookies

2 tsp baking powder

zest of 1 lemon

8 large eggs, separated

1/4 tsp cream of tartar

1 cup sugar

5 oz/145 g butter, melted

1/3 cup whole roasted hazelnuts, roughly crushed

Syrup

1 cup sugar

1/2 cup water

1/3 cup dark rum

Method

1 In a food processor, blend together the hazelnuts and cookies until finely ground. Add the baking powder and zest, and pulse briefly.

2 Beat the egg whites with the cream of tartar until soft peaks form, then continue beating while adding 4 tablespoons of the sugar, 1 at a time. Once the sugar has been added and dissolved, the whites should be stiff and glossy.

3 In a clean bowl, beat together the egg yolks and the remaining sugar until the mixture is thick and pale. Fold the nut mixture into the yolks, then add the melted butter, and stir thoroughly to combine. Pour the cake batter on top of the whites and gently fold together using a spatula.

4 Spoon the cake batter into a greased and floured 12 in x 8 in/30 cm x 20 cm cake tin or metal baking dish, then sprinkle the remaining nuts over the top.

5 Bake at 350°F/180°C/Gas Mark 4 for 40 minutes or until no longer 'wobbly' in the center.

6 Meanwhile, make the syrup. Bring the sugar and water to the boil and simmer for 5 minutes. Add the rum and continue boiling for 3 more minutes, then set aside to cool.

7 When the cake has finished cooking, remove from the oven and pour over the warm syrup. Allow to cool, then cut into diamond shapes (like baklava). Serve with a little extra syrup drizzled over.

Note: The easiest way to cut a rectangular cake into diamonds is as follows: First, cut 3 or 4 strips of cake from 1 end of the tin to the other. Then, hold your knife at a 45 degree angle and cut further strips diagonally across the tin.

Serves 10–12

Green Tea Tiramisu Flavored with Sambucca

Ingredients

7 oz/200 g marscapone

1½ tbsp Tia Maria

2 eggs

1½ tbsp superfine sugar

1½ tbsp green tea powder

2 tbsp sambucca

1½ tbsp sugar

¼ cup water

2 pieces sponge cake 8 x 8 in/20 x 20cm
and ¾ in/2 cm thick

fresh berries to serve

Method

1 Stir together the marscapone and Tia Maria. Separate the eggs and beat the egg yolks and superfine sugar until light and fluffy.

2 Beat the egg whites until soft peaks form. Gently fold in the marscapone mixture and beaten egg yolks.

3 Place the green tea, sambucca, sugar, and water in a small saucepan and stir over a medium heat until the sugar has dissolved.

4 Place a layer of sponge on the base of a square dish. Pour over ½ the green tea syrup, then spread with ½ the marscapone mixture. Top with the remaining sponge, the syrup, and the marscapone mixture. Refrigerate for 4 hours or overnight.

5 Carefully cut into 8 triangles. Serve with a sprinkle of green tea powder and some fresh berries.

Serves 4

Ice Cream Christmas Pudding

Ingredients

4 cups chocolate ice cream, softened

4 oz/115 g candied apricots, chopped

4 oz/115 g candied cherries, chopped

4 oz/115 g candied pears, chopped

3 oz/85 g golden raisins

2¹/₂ oz/75 g raisins, chopped

2 tbsp rum

rum custard to serve

Method

1 Place the ice cream, apricots, cherries, pears, golden raisins, raisins, and rum in a bowl, and mix to combine. Pour into an oiled and lined 6 cup capacity pudding basin.

2 Freeze for 3 hours or until firm. To serve, slice the pudding and serve with the rum custard.

Note: To help unmold the pudding, briefly hold a warm damp kitchen towel around the outside of the mold. To serve, slice the pudding and serve with rum custard.

Serves 8

Indian Yogurt Banana Cake

Ingredients

3 oz/85 g dried coconut, toasted

4¹/₂ oz/125 g ghee

5 oz/145 g superfine sugar

1¹/₂ oz/45 g brown sugar

2 large eggs

3 medium large bananas, very ripe

7 oz/200 g thick plain yogurt

9 oz/255 g all-purpose flour

¹/₂ tsp baking powder

1 tsp cinnamon

¹/₂ tsp apple spice

7 oz/200 g sour cream

3¹/₂ oz/100 g confectioners' sugar

¹/₄ cup toasted shredded coconut

Method

1 Preheat the oven to 375°F/190°C/Gas Mark 5. Remove the base from a 8¹/₂–9¹/₂ in/22–24 cm nonstick springform tin and place a piece of baking paper over the top. Replace the sides of the tin, causing the paper to form a false base. Grease the tin and pour in the toasted dried coconut. Tip the tin all around to coat the greased sides with the coconut, then pour out the excess and reserve for the cake batter.

2 Beat the ghee and sugars in a bowl until creamy, then add the eggs, 1 at a time, beating well after each addition. Meanwhile, mash the bananas.

3 Remove the bowl from the mixer, then add the mashed bananas, yogurt, flour, baking powder, cinnamon, spice, and remaining coconut and stir thoroughly with a wooden spoon until all the ingredients are well combined and no floury areas remain.

4 Spoon the mixture into the prepared tin and gently smooth the top.

5 Bake for 55 minutes, or until firm and 'springy' when depressed in the center of the cake. Remove from the oven, allow to cool for 15 minutes, then remove the sides of the tin and cool completely. When cool, remove the base and baking paper and place the cake on a platter.

6 To make the icing, mix together the sour cream and confectioners' sugar until thick and spreadable, then spread over the top of the cool cake. Pour the shredded coconut over the cream, until thickly covered.

Serves 8–10

Italian Refrigerator Cake

Ingredients

4 oz/115 g all-purpose flour

3/4 tsp baking powder

1/4 tsp salt

2 egg yolks

4 fl oz/115 mL cold water

7 oz/200 g superfine sugar

1 tsp vanilla extract

1/2 tsp lemon extract

2 egg whites

Filling and Icing

2 oz/55 g chocolate chips

5 oz/145 g superfine sugar

1 lb/455 g ricotta or cheese curd

1/2 tsp ground cloves

2 tbsp grated lemon rind

2 tbsp grated orange rind

2 tbsp sweet vermouth

Method

1 Sift the flour, baking powder, and salt together. Beat the egg yolks and water until fluffy and treble in volume. Add the sugar gradually and continue beating until light and thick.

2 Stir in the vanilla and lemon extract, then add the flour mixture all at once, folding it in with a rubber spatula or a metal spoon.

3 Whisk the egg whites until stiff peaks form, and fold into the mixture. Place in 2 greased and lined 8 in/20 cm sandwich tins and bake in a preheated moderate oven at 350°F/180°C/Gas Mark 4 for 20–25 minutes.

4 Invert the tins on wire racks and leave until they are cold. Remove the tins and lining paper.

5 Melt the chocolate chips in a bowl over hot water. Stir in the sugar and the remaining ingredients, except the vermouth, and mix well. Chill in the refrigerator for 30 minutes before using. Put 1 cake layer onto a serving plate. Sprinkle with 1/2 the vermouth and spread with less than 1/2 the filling. Top with a second layer and sprinkle with the remaining vermouth and then spread the filling over the top and sides of the cake using a palette knife. Smooth the filling.

6 Chill for about 4 hours before serving. You can decorate the cake with whipped cream just before serving or serve with a bowl of whipped cream handed round separately.

Serves 8

Lebanese Tahina Cake

Ingredients

3 tbsp sesame seeds

1 cup tahina (sesame seed paste)

3/4 cup superfine sugar

1/4 cup brown sugar

grated rind and juice of 2 oranges

7 oz/200 g thick plain yogurt

2 1/2 cups all-purpose flour

2 1/2 tsp baking powder

1/2 tsp salt

1 tsp apple spice

3 1/2 oz/100 g chopped pistachios

3 tbsp sesame seeds, additional

6 dates, stones removed and
   flesh chopped

Method

1 Grease a 9 1/2 in/24 cm cake tin generously and sprinkle with the 3 tablespoons of sesame seeds. Set aside. Preheat the oven to 325°F/170°C/Gas Mark 3.

2 In the bowl of an electric mixer, beat the tahina, superfine sugar, brown sugar, and orange rind until thick and creamy. Add the orange juice and yogurt. Continue to beat until combined.

3 Fold in the flour, baking powder, salt, apple spice, pistachio nuts, sesame seeds, and chopped dates and mix thoroughly by hand until all ingredients are well mixed and distributed.

4 Spoon the batter into the prepared cake tin and smooth the top. Bake for 45 minutes, or until the cake is firm to the touch. Turn the cake out of the tin and allow to cool.

Serves 8–10

329

Louisiana Banana Cake

Ingredients

Cake

2 cups all-purpose flour

¼ cup corn starch

2 tsp baking powder

I tsp baking soda

½ tsp nutmeg

7 oz/200 g butter, softened

I cup brown sugar

3 eggs

2 tsp vanilla extract

¾ cup buttermilk

3 medium bananas, mashed

½ cup toasted pine nuts

½ cup shredded coconut

Frosting

7 oz/200 g butter

3 cups confectioners' sugar

2 small ripe bananas, mashed

¼ cup dark rum

½ tsp cinnamon

I tbsp vanilla extract

I tbsp fresh lemon juice

I½ cups toasted shredded coconut

Method

1 Preheat the oven to 375°F/190°C/Gas Mark 5 and butter a 9½ in/24 cm springform, nonstick cake tin or 9 x 5 in/23 x 13 cm loaf tin.

2 In a large bowl, combine the flour, corn starch, baking powder, baking soda, and nutmeg. Set aside.

3 Beat the butter and sugar together until light and fluffy, then add the eggs and vanilla extract, and mix thoroughly. In a separate bowl, mix the buttermilk and mashed bananas.

4 Add ½ the flour mixture to the creamed sugar, then add ½ the buttermilk/banana mixture. Mix thoroughly, then add the remaining flour mixture and buttermilk/banana mixture, and mix very well. Add the pine nuts and coconut and stir to distribute.

5 Pour the batter into the prepared cake tin and bake for 50 minutes, or until the cake is 'springy' in the center when gently pressed. Remove the cake from the oven and cool in the tin for 30 minutes, then remove the cake from the tin and cool completely.

6 To make the frosting, beat the softened butter and confectioners' sugar together until thick and pale, then fold through the bananas, rum, cinnamon, vanilla, and lemon juice. Beat well to combine, then spread over the top of the cooled cake. Generously sprinkle the coconut over the cake, covering the frosting thoroughly.

Serves 8–10

Russian Cheesecake

Ingredients

Crust

3 tbsp sugar

3 tbsp brown sugar

1/2 tsp nutmeg

3 tbsp butter, softened

3/4 cup ground walnuts

3/4 cup all-purpose flour

1 tsp baking powder

Cheesecake

1 1/2 lb/700 g creamed cheese, softened

7 oz/200 g soft white cheese such as ricotta

1 1/2 cups sugar

6 large eggs, separated

juice and zest of 1 large lemon

3 tbsp all-purpose flour

1 cup thick cream

1 cup golden raisins, optional

2 tbsp confectioners' sugar

Method

1 Preheat the oven to 400°F/200°C/Gas Mark 6 and butter a 11 in/28 cm nonstick springform cake tin. Remove the base of the cake tin from the sides and lay a piece baking paper over the base. Replace the sides to hold the paper in place.

2 First, prepare the crust. Using a food processor or blender, pulse together all the 'crust' ingredients until a stiff dough forms. Roll out the dough and press over the base of the cake tin. Bake for 10 minutes, then remove from the oven and cool.

3 Meanwhile, in a large bowl of an electric mixer, combine the creamed cheese, white cheese, and 1 cup of sugar, and beat for 3 minutes or until the mixture is smooth. Add the egg yolks 1 at a time, beating well after each addition. Add the juice and zest of the lemon and the all-purpose flour, and mix until combined.

4 In a separate bowl, beat the egg whites until foaming, then add the remaining 1/2 cup of the sugar, sprinkling the sugar into the egg whites while the motor is running. When all the sugar has been added, raise the speed of the mixer to the fastest, then allow the egg whites to beat until they are thick and glossy.

5 In a separate bowl, beat the cream until soft peaks form. Fold the beaten cream and the egg whites into the cheese mixture and combine thoroughly. Pour the batter into the cooled crust, then sprinkle the golden raisins, if using, over the batter, and gently stir a few in so that they drop below the surface.

6 Bake for 10 minutes, then reduce the heat to 300°F/150°C/Gas Mark 2 and cook for 1 hour. Turn off the oven heat and leave the cake in the oven undisturbed. When the cake has cooled, remove from the oven and chill overnight. Transfer the cake to a platter, then gently ease the paper out from under the cake. Sprinkle with the confectioners' sugar and serve.

Serves 10–12

Index